TURN ON HOPE STREET

Stories, Faith and

Neuroscience

ROSIE CLANDOS

In honor of my dad, Bruno (Barney) Zoladz

and my mom, Mary Natalie Vujnovich Zoladz

Dedicated

To my family and friends

and to those who struggle to live fuller, happier lives

Contents

Forward

In 2008, I was writing an article for the *Los Angeles Times* about learning and stress. One of the neuroscientists I interviewed was Eric Kandel, M.D., a Nobel Laureate who studied memory storage in brain cells.

He explained that repeated thoughts, words, and actions related to fear, stress, and anxiety can change the structure and function of the brain. In the same way, the brain's structure and function can be changed by hope, love, and happiness. [1]

Did I hear right? This was exciting news.

Neuroplasticity was coming into public awareness at that time, and I wanted to confirm my understanding of it. I rephrased my question. Same answer, different wording. By the third time, Kandel was laughing. When I got off the phone, I was dancing.

I imagined that neuroplasticity was like walking on a path in the woods. If I frequently walked on that path, it would become wider, and the ground would be firmer.

Neuroplasticity explained a lot in my life – the impact of environment, choices, nurturing, and trauma. Neuroplasticity also helped me understand the power of prayer and having a spiritual connection. And that knowledge gave me hope.

For years, I had been saying all kinds of prayers, for all kinds of reasons, and in all kinds of ways. Some of my prayers were answered – others were not. The news about neuroplasticity helped me understand that my brain and behavior can actually *change* when I pray frequently with confidence and hope.

Changes in our brains occur at different rates. Rapid changes can happen during highly emotional situations or events. Changes also occur quickly when injury or disease is involved. Otherwise, long-term changes often happen slowly. To change faster, we can frequently think about positive experiences and apply the lessons to other situations.

I used to think that praying mostly involved asking or begging God to *change* a negative situation, or to *help me* solve a problem, or to *give* me something. But maybe I could also express more gratitude. Gratitude primes the brain for hope and promotes changes.

In addition to changing ourselves, we may affect people around us. For example, when we show empathy or compassion, then certain neurons are understood to trigger similar, "contagious" emotions in most people.[2] When many people watch a sad movie, they also feel sad. But seeing or hearing other strong emotions – such as fear and hate – can be contagious, too.

Prayer is simply talking to God, and it involves belief or hope. For some people, that's easy, possibly because of their biology or life experiences. Other people may need to try very hard to believe and imagine a positive outcome.

Optimism can be more effective and healthier than *only* pleading for answers to our prayers. There is a lot of research about the health benefits of optimism. For example, having a positive emotional style has been shown to predict resistance to colds and viruses.[3] Also, optimism plays a crucial role in self-care and the management of chronic illness.[4] Further, having positive beliefs about aging can reduce stress and act as a protective factor, even for people at high risk of dementia.[5]

This book is based on my belief that God has given each of us a brain and the responsibility to think, evaluate information, and make

12

decisions. By understanding more about the brain, anyone can use this gift more effectively.

Ultimately, we have the option to choose and believe *anything* – good or bad. We can justify whatever we want to believe – or whatever we are led to believe. Consider the past: Some people used the Bible to justify slavery. Others used the same Bible to condemn it.

And with that comes another sobering point. Neuroscientist Kandel grew up in Austria, and he was nine years old when Nazis took over the country in 1938. After his non-Jewish friends and classmates heard repeated messages of hate, they would become his tormentors.[6]

For good or evil – that's neuroplasticity.

Introduction and Explainer

I realize people have different views on religion and social issues. But surprisingly, many world religions and thoughtful practices share the same core values, such as – truth, kindness, gratitude, generosity, peace, self-control, and patience. This book is about benefiting from those values. It's also about the benefits of praying, or simply talking to God, and experiencing more hope. These benefits are not superficial optimism. They are science. And I've simplified the science here.

You may be reading this because you want more hope. Or you may be looking for better health, or your loved ones may be facing challenges. No matter what your reasons are for choosing this book, I expect you'll want to get the most benefits from reading it. So here are some suggestions.

Apply the information

The greatest benefits from reading any book will occur when we *do* something with new information. If we practice, talk, write, think, or associate the new information to what we already know, then tiny fibers (*dendrites*) grow on our brain cells. They connect to other brain cells. New brain pathways are created, and memories are formed.[1] Then it's easier to recall and use the information to improve our lives.

I suggest making a mess of this book. Write in it, note your questions and comments. Use it as a workbook and log your ideas or personal experiences.

Each chapter in this book contains three short sections: stories, science, and inspiration. These separate sections were created to improve memory, learning, and emotional impact. The personal stories are true. The science section provides more information related to the chapter topics. The inspirational references and affirmations are those I've used in tough times, and they are based on my faith background. Your background may be different, so space is provided for your own inspirational quotes or affirmations. At the end of some chapters, you'll find a supplementary section with practical tips.

Find support

Disbelief and cynicism from some people can diminish my confidence when I'm praying or speaking optimistically. I may feel foolish or doubt myself. But we have a choice to ignore skepticism and focus on our goals. We can find people who are interested in building hope and practicing common values or virtues.

Naturally, we find encouragement in traditions or choices that resonate with us. For some individuals such as myself, Jesus provided great support on the topic of hope. He is reported to have told his followers to ask for *anything* they need, believe it will be received, persist, and thank God in advance. That's a wild claim. But there's a catch.

He told people to *first* forgive others, so their own mistakes can be forgiven. He commanded people to love each other. And he said to "abide" in him. For me, that means resisting unhealthy distractions and honestly expressing my thoughts and feelings to him. The process naturally includes using my conscience, intuition, and reasoning. When I talk to God as a friend, I experience a sense of

15

love and hope. In the end, my prayers are answered, refined, or redirected. But sometimes they're not answered. Then I'm compelled to reconnect with more questions and honest emotions. This process eventually provides comfort, guidance, or insight.

Whether or not you have a faith tradition, you can use similar approaches. Anyone can ask, believe, persist, and be thankful. Anyone can practice forgiveness, admit their faults, and love others. All of us can work to refuse unhealthy distractions. We can tell the truth and use our intuition and conscience. If we need more help or encouragement, we can reach out to additional resources – faith-based or secular.

Know the benefits

Practicing these common values can have a positive impact on the body, brain, emotions, and behavior. Thinking loving thoughts can produce oxytocin, serotonin, and dopamine – which helps to reduce pain.[2] Kindness or altruism activates the pleasure centers of the brain.[3] Forgiveness reduces physical symptoms and heart rate.[4] Expressing gratitude improves mood and benefits relationships, and it is associated with resilience after trauma.[5,6,7] Admitting faults can reduce stress, increase social trust, and improve leadership skills.[8,9,10] Refusing to be distracted by negative impulses produces dopamine to help focus on our goals.[11,12]

Also, when a person prays and perceives God as loving, then activity in the amygdala is decreased and so is anxiety or fear. Further, believing in God may cause a person to feel less stressed when they make an error.[13] In addition, spiritual practices can strengthen the anterior cingulate cortex, an area that processes intuition and empathy.

Finally, prayer or meditation can trigger the relaxation response. The process involves slowly inhaling, pausing, and then slowly exhaling while silently repeating a comforting word or phrase – either religious or secular.

The relaxation response has been shown to have a positive effect on blood pressure, heart rate, and oxygen consumption.[14] Harvard researcher Herbert Benson found that the relaxation response occurred when people prayed or meditated for 10 minutes or more.

Use affirmations

Another way to benefit from this book is to say the positive affirmations at the end of each chapter or write your own affirmations. Speaking aloud, hearing yourself, and *emphasizing* some words will engage more senses and activate more brain areas, which can improve memory and mood.[15] In addition, saying affirmations aloud can help to maintain a positive mental focus and reduce intrusive negative thoughts. In the privacy of your home or car, you may want to try using audible affirmations or prayer.

Take time

Whether we're creating new habits or waiting for prayers to be answered, patience helps. It's easy to underestimate the time needed to reach our goals and then feel disappointed. But appreciating each of our little steps toward progress can produce dopamine, which increases our motivation to reach our goals.[16]

Look and find

There's a blend of wisdom and hope in the ancient directive: "Seek and you will find." In the brain, the reticular activating system helps people focus on certain stimuli and ignore other stimuli. You buy a red car, and you start seeing more red cars on the road. You look for hope and resilience, and you start finding it.

Finally, remember you're not alone in your search. All of us test and try new ways to grow. Some people find growth in organized religion. Others avoid organized religion, yet they want a spiritual connection or science-based information for growth. Probably everyone wants a bit more peace or comfort. And then, there are those of us who simply want a second chance.

I don't claim to have all the answers, but it is my wish that we find what we need to overcome challenges as we walk together on Hope Street.

Chapter 1

Kindness vs. Harshness

My dad was a creative guy who could be helpful, thoughtful, and generous. Living in poverty during the Depression, he never graduated from high school, but he loved learning. He taught himself and his five daughters many practical things, and we were proud of his creativity and resourcefulness.

When I was an adult, my dad and I liked going to libraries together. Sometimes we would walk arm-in-arm in pretty neighborhoods outside of the industrial areas of Detroit, pretending we lived near each other in cute little houses with flower gardens.

But as I was growing up, he suffered from alcohol dependence, and if he was sick or angry, I had to be very careful.

In his 80s, he began receiving treatment for liver cancer, and the nurses said he was the model patient. But when treatment failed and he became very ill, he had a difficult time. His pain increased, he could barely eat, and he couldn't sleep.

I had been living in California, and to help my dad for a few weeks, I went back to Detroit. When I walked into his house on Valentine's Day, he angrily yelled. "What are you doing here?!"

His neighborhood was unsafe, and I couldn't park my sister's new car there overnight. He said I should stay at her house. I knew my dad cared about me. But it wasn't long before I wanted to get away from him and the memories of his temper.

Back home in California, my pastor sometimes talked about blessing people who upset us. It sounded like a good idea. I seldom did it, but I knew of other people who did. I had visited Black churches in Los Angeles and met people who had unusually strong faith, courage, and determination. In many of those churches, the style of praying was passionate and fervent. There, and in other situations, I have often seen that when the needs are greater, the faith is stronger.

That Sunday in Detroit, I sincerely needed strength, so I went to a Black church. I was inspired by the music, lyrics, and people who danced as they thanked God. After the service, three women prayed with me and encouraged me to bless my dad – just as Jesus directed people to do.

When I returned to my dad's house, he was angry and yelling in the living room. I went into the kitchen to cook his meal. I knew he couldn't hear, and I passionately repeated sentences aloud like this: "Lord, please bless my dad with peace. Please bless him with kindness…. I bless him…. *Dad, I bless you with love. You are kind and loving, Dad. You are patient….*"

By the time I brought the food to him, I felt pretty good. What happened next shocked me.

He apologized! He had never stopped and apologized in the midst of an anger storm.

"I'm so sorry, so so sorry, Rosie…. I just feel so sick…."

The immediate love and compassion I felt for him amazed me. It may have been the first time I was able to really see the pain below the surface of his angry behavior.

Later, when I looked out the living room window, his neighborhood looked different. I felt connected to it and to the people who lived there.

Looking back, I realize that talking with compassionate women produced oxytocin and trust.[1] Hearing their confident prayers increased my confidence. Blessing my dad surely reduced activity in my amygdala, the area of my brain that activates the fight-or-flight response. Experiencing positive results from my prayers must have activated the reward circuits in my brain, and it certainly influenced my expectations for future positive outcomes.[2]

What caused my dad to act unusually kind when he had been angry? I would attribute his turn-around to the power of prayer and blessings.

* * *

Unfortunately, there have been times when I was on the other side of kindness, and a wiser person would lead the way.

For a little while when I was in high school in Detroit, I worked the midnight shift at Biff's Restaurant near the Fisher Building. One night, I was very tired and wondered how I'd make it through the upcoming day. When it was near the end of my shift, a man came in and sat in a closed area of the restaurant. I explained that he'd have to sit somewhere else. He politely asked again. And again, I said no and gave him the stink eye.

The owner gently intervened, "It's OK. Let him sit there."

21

I was embarrassed.

The customer talked kindly to me as I brought him coffee, but I was still aloof. When he got up to leave, I saw that he had left a tip. It was five times larger than his bill.

The man's kindness made me feel so sad. I had to fight back my tears. He must have seen how bad I was feeling.

I wish I could have told him what his actions meant to me. Maybe he saw it in my eyes.

For years, I would savor the memory of this stranger's compassion and insight.

Chapter 1: Kindness vs. Harshness

Related Science

Our brains are designed to copy the emotional signals or expressions of people we see or hear. That means, showing compassion to a person may cause that person to also feel compassion, according to research led by Mariska Kret and published in *Frontiers in Human Neuroscience* in 2013. The study was titled "Emotional signals from faces, bodies, and scenes influence observers' face expressions, fixations, and pupil size."

* * *

Compassionate thoughts and feelings motivate people to *act* compassionately. The research by Yoni Ashar was reported in a 2016 article in *Emotion*. The study was titled "Effects of compassion meditation on a psychological model of charitable donation."

* * *

To determine how the brain heals emotional wounds, a research team led by Emiliano Ricciardi found that forgiveness activated brain networks associated with empathy. These areas involved the dorsolateral prefrontal cortex, the precuneus, and the right inferior parietal region of the brain. The research was published in *Frontiers in Human Neuroscience* in 2013. The study was titled "How the brain heals emotional wounds: the functional neuroanatomy of forgiveness."

* * *

Many of the brain's structures and functions can be permanently altered by excessive fear or anger – which can reduce our ability to properly reason and remember. In turn, these alterations affect decision-making and responses to people. The research was led by Richard J. Davidson and published in 2002 in *Biological Psychiatry.* The study was titled "Neural and behavioral substrates of mood and mood regulation."

* * *

Researcher J. Dua showed that positive thoughts can replace negative thoughts and reduce anger and frustration. The study was published 1993 in the *Journal of Genetic Psychology* and titled "Effectiveness of training in negative thought reduction and positive thought increment in reducing thought-produced distress."

Dear Reader,

Kindness is our balm and touchstone –

A place where hope begins,

A place that echoes with resilience.

We can choose to embrace the wisdom and warmth of new teachers.

Lessons are tested.

Rewards are remembered.

Always justified, compassion and kindness heals.

Rosie

Chapter 1: Kindness vs. Harshness

Inspiration and Affirmations

Anxious hearts are very heavy, but a word of encouragement does wonders. Proverbs 12:25 (TLB)

Affirmations: My encouraging words can help other people. When I'm upset, I will speak encouraging words to myself. They lighten my heart and my mood.

Write your own affirmations:

_____

_____

_____

Some people like to make cutting remarks, but the words of the wise soothe and heal. Proverbs 12:18 (TLB)

Affirmations: I will speak lovingly and kindly to others and myself. My words help to soothe and restore me and them.

Write your own affirmations:

_____

_____

_____

Pleasant words are a honeycomb, sweet to the soul and healing to the bones. Proverbs 16:24 (TLB)

Affirmations: When I speak kindly to myself and other people, I can feel pleasant and helpful.

Write your own affirmations:

_____

_____

_____

Try to show as much compassion as your Father does. Never criticize or condemn, or it will all come back on you. Luke 6:36 (TLB)

Affirmations: God is compassionate. I refuse to criticize or condemn myself or other people. I'm compassionate with myself.

Write your own affirmations:

_____

_____

_____

You must love others as much as yourself. Mark 12:31 (TLB)

Affirmations: I will love my neighbor, and I will love myself. If I can't love myself, how can I love anyone else?

Write your own affirmations:

_____

_____

_____

You were called to be free. But do not use your freedom to indulge the flesh; rather, serve one another in love. Galatians 5:13 (NIV)

Affirmations: I can experience a sense of freedom when I help people and show love to others.

Write your own affirmations:

_____

_____

_____

Your own soul is nourished when you are kind. Proverbs 11:17 (TLB)

Affirmations: I will be kind to myself and others. Kindness nourishes my soul, my mind, and my body. I refuse to be mean to myself or others. And I will feel better when I speak kindly to myself.

Write your own affirmations:

_____

_____

_____

[Jesus said] "Pray like this: 'Our Father in heaven, may your name be kept holy. May your Kingdom come soon. May your will be done on earth, as it is in heaven. Give us today the food we need, and forgive us our sins, as we have forgiven those who sin against us. And don't let us yield to temptation but rescue us from the evil one.'" Matthew 6:9-13 (NLT)

Affirmations: Dear God, you are holy. I pray that your will is done in my life and in this world. Please provide what I need today. And please forgive me, just as I forgive others. Help me refuse to do the things that are wrong or unwise.

Write your own affirmations:

_____

_____

_____

Chapter 2

Forgiveness vs. Anger

Shortly after the World Trade Center was attacked on September 11, 2001, I was in a prayer meeting and a challenging question came to mind. The question was based on instructions attributed to Jesus: Pray for your enemies. Bless those who curse you.

I asked the pastor, "Should we be praying for the terrorists?" He gave me a dirty look. Still, I wondered: *How* could anyone pray for them?

I would base my own answer on the following events. When I was 21, I moved from Detroit to Los Angeles. On my first Saturday there, I ate dinner in a restaurant and chatted for a long time with the people next to me.

Walking back to my hotel room and passing lovely homes, I was so happy to see that trees in L.A. still had leaves, and flowers were still blooming at Thanksgiving time.

That evening, a traumatic event happened to me – an armed robbery and rape. Police drove me to a hospital.

The next morning, I met with a therapist and expressed my fear, sadness, and hatred. I expressed those feelings for months. As time passed, frequently thinking about the trauma would reactivate the fight-or-flight response and increase my stress hormones.

Three years later, I walked into the small lobby of my office building, and I heard a commotion. I saw my co-worker with her head bent down on her desk. She was saying, "I can't see you. I don't know what you look like."

Just then, two men stepped out from behind a wall. One guy had a small gun. (I thought it wasn't real.) He tried to yank my wallet from my hand. Furious, I struggled with him. He got away with the wallet, nothing else.

The following year I received an envelope without a return address. The only thing inside the envelope was a small picture of my disabled sister Patty with her high school graduation cap.

On the other side of the picture was a message she had written in her wiggly handwriting. Her picture along with some ID and five dollars were the only things that had been in my stolen wallet.

I often wondered if the man felt sorry when he saw the picture of Patty. When I'd imagine him feeling some empathy for my sister, I'd have a slight feeling of kindness for him.

One day I had a thought about praying for him. I decided to pray that the man wouldn't rob other people. One thought led to another, and this new thought was about the perpetrator who had attacked me three years earlier. But I refused to even consider praying for him.

Forgiveness has various meanings, some confusing. For me, forgiveness eventually came to mean *for-giving*. I thought of a way to *give* the man something relevant. (This is tricky – please stay with me here.) I *gave* him a blessing so he would have compassion for other women. I *gave* him a blessing so he would have self-control.

31

And I *gave* him a blessing so he would get appropriate treatment. I gave those blessings to *change* the man's behavior and to *protect* other women. This was not easy. But it was empowering. And my blessings *gave me* something – peace.

Looking back, I realized that giving the man this relevant blessing decreased activity in my amygdala and thwarted the fight-or-flight response. Plus, the blessing surely increased activity in brain areas related to my empowerment and self-control.[1] I wonder if that's why we are directed to pray for our enemies and bless those who curse us. We're not directed to simply ask God to bless them. There's a big difference and a big benefit.

* * *

Recently, I asked someone about the secret of her 30-year marriage. "Pick your battles," she said.

Then she asked if I was married, and if I had a secret. I'm not married anymore, but I do have a secret. This is my post-marriage secret: When you're upset about your partner's (or anyone's) behavior, express your deepest feelings to God. Then bless them with the opposite behavior. This can help you also and give you a fresh perspective along with clarity and hope.

I do not suggest just a short, measly prayer. No, no. Better yet, try a spoken prayer – so you can hear yourself, and a prayer that involves physical movement, such as walking or housework. Then electrical energy can shift more easily from your amygdala to other brain areas that process reasoning, empathy, and forgiveness.[2]

To overcome recurrent negative memories, I suggest repeating those prayers and blessings. Forgiveness often happens in layers. Of course, deal with the issues. But repetitive negative thoughts can magnify problems, even when those thoughts are random or triggered by other events. Nevertheless, your prayers and blessings can change you and your relationships.

I've often wondered what would have happened if I had prayed in this way for important people in my past. Would my prayers and blessings have activated certain neurons in them and triggered similar emotions and empathy? In turn, would they have felt more compassion toward me? Who knows?

On a broader level, who knows what might happen to people mentioned in disturbing news reports. For example, corrupt leaders, fallen pastors, criminals, or those who promote hate or harm.

Would our prayers and blessings alleviate our feelings of anger, fear, or sadness? Would our prayers help to direct our actions more effectively? Would God – or could God – give others self-control, humility, empathy, honesty, or any other virtue that is the opposite of their destructive choices and actions?

We all have free will. Yet, I want to believe – I have to believe – that God could intervene in *some* way.

In the meantime, I can follow that unusual directive to boldly ask and pray for *anything* – justice, peace, and any other remedy from the Power greater than ourselves.

Chapter 2: Forgiveness vs. Anger

Related Science

War survivors and violent-crime victims who forgive those responsible for their pain have decreased depression and anxiety. The 2004 study by Alistair Spiers was published in *Australasian Psychiatry*, and it was titled "Forgiveness as a secondary prevention strategy for victims of interpersonal crime."

* * *

Expressions of compassion or empathy can reduce aggression or conflict in relationships, according to a 1994 study led by Deborah R. Richardson and published in *Aggressive Behavior*. The study was titled, "Empathy as a cognitive inhibitor of interpersonal aggression."

* * *

In a study led by Daniel Lim and published in *Emotion* in 2016, researchers found that people who experienced severe adversities were more likely to feel compassion and empathize with other people in stressful situations. The more compassion they felt, the more they did for other people. The study was titled: "Suffering and compassion. The links among adverse life experiences, empathy, compassion, and prosocial behavior."

Dear Reader,

Forgiving the unforgivable,

Who is the tormented soul?

Strengthened by forgiveness and blessings,

the fibers of the heart recover.

Braver, more resilient than we ever imagined –

We heal, we hope, and we move on.

Rosie

Chapter 2: Forgiveness vs. Anger

Inspiration and Affirmations

Love your enemies and pray for those who persecute you. Matthew 5:43 (NIV)

Affirmations: I will pray for people who upset me. I remember that when I bless them, I feel better. When it's very hard to forgive someone who hurt me, I can bless them with compassion for me and others.

Write your own affirmations:

_____

_____

_____

Do not be overcome by evil but overcome evil with good. Romans 12:21 (TLB)

Affirmations: By forgiving people or blessing them, I will overcome revenge, hatred, and bitterness.

Write your own affirmations:

_____

_____

_____

The Lord works righteousness for those who are oppressed. Psalm 103:6 (NIV)

Affirmations: I choose to believe God will help me resolve problems and provide justice.

Write your own affirmations:

_____

_____

_____

Then Peter came to him and asked, "Sir, how many times shall I forgive a brother who sins against me? Seven times?"

"No!" Jesus replied. "Seventy times seven!" Matthew 18:21 (TLB)

Affirmations: I remember that God has forgiven me countless times. So, I will forgive other people.

Write your own affirmations:

_____

_____

_____

When you stand praying, if you hold anything against anyone, forgive them, so that your Father in heaven may forgive you your sins. Mark 11:25 (NIV)

Affirmations: I will forgive people who have offended me or hurt me. And I know I've offended or hurt other people.

Write your own affirmations:

_____

_____

_____

When you obey me, you are living in my love, just as I obey my Father and live in his love. John 15:10 (TLB)

Affirmations: When I obey God's instructions and listen to my conscience, I can feel God's love.

Write your own affirmations:

_____

_____

_____

Chapter 3

Gratitude vs. Bitterness

In West Hollywood, I used to eat in a deli where the man working behind the counter joked with customers in his Eastern European accent.

One day I asked him, "How can you be so friendly all the time?"

"Why do you ask?"

His shirt sleeve was rolled up, and I could see the imprint made in a Nazi concentration camp.

"You have numbers on your arm," I said softly.

He stretched out his arms and said, "I'm alive! I make a choice to be happy!"

* * *

I visited my 30-year-old sister Patty in Detroit while she was living in a nursing home. She was born with mild cerebral palsy and later developed hydrocephalus. Water pressure slowly accumulated on Patty's brain, and the fluid eventually enlarged her head which caused serious problems. My mom struggled with fear and many medical decisions. She also suffered with distrust and anger. Surgery was discouraged, as Patty wasn't expected to live beyond age five.

When Patty was 21, her headaches were unbearable, and she chose to have a shunt inserted into her head to relieve the water pressure. An infection occurred. The shunt was removed. Problems continued. Patty lived with my mom for a while, and then she moved to a nursing home in Detroit.

When Patty was 30, the hallways in the nursing home had lost-looking patients, bad smells, and cockroaches. When I entered Patty's room, she was surprised and immediately turned to a picture of Jesus on her wall and whispered, "Thank you."

Under the picture, there was a box of expensive chocolates that someone had given her. Patty *loved* chocolates.

After ten days, I needed to return to Los Angeles. We cried and hugged. Patty kept thanking me for visiting her.

When I finally turned away to leave, Patty called me back.

"Here, take this." It was her box of chocolates.

"I can't. No, you keep it."

"Please, please, you have to take it."

Back and forth we went. She finally demanded that I take the chocolates. In all my life, I have never received such a generous gift.

I always hoped that Patty felt even a little bit of comfort knowing she had given me so much.

* * *

Patty often called and begged me to move her to California. The Internet wasn't available at that time, and it was taking me a long time to find the right nursing home that could meet her needs and would accept her.

One day I spoke to Patty, and she sounded fine. But when we spoke a few days later, her words were garbled. The staff said she was obstinate because she refused to move her arm. I frantically tried to get a physician to examine her. After a week, he finally came to see Patty. She had had a stroke.

A social worker in Los Angeles encouraged me to do everything possible to quickly move Patty and my mom to California. After actively searching everywhere in Los Angeles County for 14 months – receiving acceptances and then refusals – we finally found a nursing home for 31-year-old Patty.

To relieve the water pressure in her brain, we quickly arranged for a UCLA neurosurgeon to meet her. He expressed strong concern that areas of her brain would collapse if another surgery were to be performed now. Surgical treatment was not recommended. Tragically, pressure would ultimately destroy major parts of Patty's brain.

* * *

At Patty's new nursing home, we met psychologist Stan Peterson. The staff and patients loved him. Exuberant and encouraging, he would get excited about the patients' smallest accomplishments. No victory was too small for him to acknowledge. One patient could tie his shoes, another patient could color, someone else could drink from a cup.

Patty and I didn't know what to make of his over-the-top attitude.

41

She smirked and rolled her eyes, struggling to say, "Is...that guy...for real...or what?!"

One day we learned the reason for Stan's optimism and compliments to the patients.

He told me that he'd been in a serious motorcycle accident when he was 21. Months after he came out of the coma, he had total amnesia. He didn't recognize his mother or anyone else. He needed to relearn everything, including the alphabet.

After a lot of hard work, Stan went back to college, earned a doctorate degree, and became a psychologist. He counseled patients who had brain injuries, worked with family members, and supported the medical staff. His extreme appreciation finally made sense to us.

Stan would become a role model for my visits to nursing homes and for appreciating the joy of life's smallest victories. I later realized that watching Stan encourage patients and seeing the patients' gratitude must have activated the reward region of my brain, motivating me to be more of an encourager.

* * *

When Patty's condition worsened, she was moved to a different nursing home. With other problems, Patty was now blind and fed through a tube. She rarely spoke and could move only one arm.

Rosanna was Patty's nursing assistant. She spoke lovingly, and she tenderly cared for Patty – as if Patty were a princess. Every day, Rosanna dispensed blessings like they were essential medicines.

"Patty smiled today. It's a blessing!" Rosanna said. "Patty held my hand today. It's a blessing!"

Rosanna's words became ingrained.

Long after Patty had passed over to a better life at age 55, Rosanna's appreciation for any little bit of progress – any little bit of effort – resonated in my life.

* * *

After my sister died, I spent a year feeling very angry with God. I thought deeply about pain and suffering, and about my sister and others who suffer greatly. Like many people, I've heard various opinions from people who try to explain why bad things happen. I don't have all the answers, but I can't believe God wanted Patty to suffer, or that he would want other people to suffer through horrible events like the Holocaust, slavery, and wars. I believe that God *allows* everyone to have free will. But *not* everything that happens is God's will.

We have choices, and some people make bad ones. Accidents, illnesses, and mistakes happen. Disasters occur. Wars are started.

We pick up the pieces. We try to find something decent and good.

Some of my beliefs were strengthened after Patty's death. I believe God wants us to be well. Jesus never made anyone sick. He only healed people.

I believe in hope – and sometimes pain has given me defiant hope. I believe that God is with us in our terrible times. Just as he was with Patty.

It's a blessing.

Chapter 3: Gratitude vs. Bitterness

Related Science

Gratitude decreases depression and anxiety. In a study involving 224 patients, researchers assessed chronic pain, sleep disturbances, depression, anxiety, and gratitude. The results showed that gratitude helped to reduce depression. Also, there was a positive link between sleep, gratitude, and reduced anxiety. Mei-Yee Ng led the 2013 study published in the *Journal of Health Psychology*. The study was titled "The differential effects of gratitude and sleep on psychological distress in patients with chronic pain."

* * *

Oxytocin is a powerful neurotransmitter that is believed to influence social interactions and promote social bonds. Researchers found that variations in a certain gene can affect oxytocin secretion in the brain. The combination of oxytocin, genetics, and gratitude-related actions and feelings can play important roles in meaningful and significant relationships. The 2014 study led by Sara B. Algoe was published in *Social Cognitive and Affective Neuroscience*. The study is titled "Evidence for a role of the oxytocin system, indexed by genetic variation in CD38, in the social bonding effects of expressed gratitude."

* * *

People can change their mood by using their memories. Remembering positive events or situations can increase the production of the feel-good chemical serotonin in the anterior cingulate cortex. The 2007 article was published in the *Journal of Psychiatry & Neuroscience*. The article is titled, "How to increase serotonin in the human brain without drugs."

44

Dear Reader,

Hope and gratitude can make life bearable.

The fierce prayer can sustain us.

The charitable smile, touch, or story can connect us.

No matter the depth of the injuries or losses,

human endurance is strengthened by hope and gratitude.

Love bears all things. Hopes all things. Endures all things.

Love never ends.

Rosie

Chapter 3: Gratitude vs. Bitterness

Inspiration and Affirmations

Say "thank you" to the Lord for being so good, for always being so loving and kind. Has the Lord redeemed you? Then speak out! Tell others he has saved you from your enemies. Psalm 107:1 (TLB)

Affirmations: I talk about my gratitude for God's healing, help, and hope.

Write your own affirmations:

_____

_____

_____

Sing and make music in your heart to the Lord, always give thanks to God for everything, in the name of our Lord Jesus Christ. Ephesians 5:20 (NIV)

Affirmations: I express gratitude to God by singing, writing, and dancing. I thank God for helping me overcome challenges.

Write your own affirmations:

_____

_____

_____

Give thanks to the Lord, call on his name; make known among the nations what he has done. Psalms 105:1 (NIV)

Affirmations: I enjoy thanking God for all the wonderful things he does, and I tell people about his love and kindness.

Write your own affirmations:

_____

_____

_____

Give thanks in all circumstances, for this is God's will for you in Christ Jesus. 1 Thessalonians 5:18 (NIV)

Affirmations: I look for ways to be thankful, even in difficult times. I believe that with God's help, I find make something good come from something bad.

Write your own affirmations:

_____

_____

_____

Death and life are in the power of the tongue, and those who chose it, will eat its fruit. Proverbs 18:21 (NLV)

Affirmations: I know that what I say has the power to build or destroy. I have a choice to speak with hate or love, despair or hope, bitterness or gratitude.

Write your own affirmations:

_____

_____

_____

His purpose was for the nations to seek after God and perhaps feel their way toward him and find him – though he is not far from any one of us. Acts 17:27 (NLT)

Affirmations: I can feel my way – or fumble my way – toward God and gratitude. I will refuse to be bitter. I choose to be grateful that God is near me.

Write your own affirmations:

_____

_____

_____

Chapter 4

Truth vs. Deception

I know we've all done embarrassing things. I've done a lot of them – especially during my 20s.

I'm not going to talk much about the night I went out dancing and woke up in the morning with an inflated ego about my "talent." Then one of my friends invited me to an open audition for dancers at the Burbank movie studios. Oh, she *knew* we'd get picked because she had friends in show business!

I was OK with the jazz-dance segment, but I won't go into detail about how I tried to tap dance *without* tap shoes and *without* ever having taken even one tap-dancing lesson.

No, I won't talk much about the movie people who covered their laughing mouths and the 200-plus *real* dancers who were probably snickering as I did my rendition of tap dancing while making big circles with my arms like a three-year-old.

And I'll just hint about the puny and fumbling basketball team I organized in Hollywood. Many of the women had never played team sports. Our team always had embarrassing losses. But before playing the best team in the league, our anxiety turned to giddiness.

We pumped up our bravado and promised to really *focus* on the ball this time. Amazingly, we won the game.

Instead of a story that I eventually laughed about, I'll share an embarrassing story about misplaced trust. It's a story about truth, lies, and neuroplasticity. But it's also a story about resilience.

* * *

When I was 21, I was looking for ways to improve myself, and I signed up for a six-month program in Los Angeles. At that time, new types of therapies were touting novel approaches and promising results.

As the program gradually evolved and lengthened, close friendships grew. Shared living arrangements morphed into a neighborhood community. Many people enjoyed the benefits of the program and the social life – parties, team sports, and traveling together. Other people had different experiences. Over time, problems were brewing.

When some counselors and group members exposed unethical and exploitative actions of certain therapists, the idealistic beliefs were shattered, and the community ended. A major lawsuit occurred, and professional licenses were lost.

I wondered how a group that included professionals – physicians, lawyers, and educators – could essentially excuse or ignore unethical practices.

I realized that personal needs or fear can silence a person – so can the potential loss of benefits: friendships, familiarity, community, status, or money. Sometimes smart people can act like they're ignorant. Observant people can act like they're blind. Yet, we are *all* born with an Achilles heel, a weakness or susceptibility that can be exploited.

I also realized that the persuasive speech of charismatic and tenacious people in leadership roles can cause others to overestimate authority or expertise. In group settings, sometimes contagious emotions can reduce critical thinking, regardless of a person's education or professional status.

In other realms, a similar and more common process is called "groupthink." Scholars explain that it happens when members of tight in-groups strive for unity, while they fail to realistically assess situations. The outcome is irrational thinking and poor decision-making.

The groupthink process was linked to NASA's role in the Challenger Space Shuttle explosion, and President Kennedy's mistake to invade Cuba (Bay of Pigs Invasion), and other disasters or fiascos involving intelligent, successful people. [1]

In Los Angeles, the once-promising therapy received news coverage, and I was concerned that people would fail to understand the common thinking traps which could affect anyone.

I learned that those thinking traps had a name: *logical fallacies*. They were the half-truths and emotional appeals that triggered fear or false hope. They were the excuses to make unreasonable actions sound reasonable. They were the demeaning comments or deliberate distractions from important questions. They were the subtle manipulations that enabled and empowered organization leaders.

Afterward, I explicitly understood the phenomenon of group mentality. To better evaluate future choices, I would ask more questions and identify logical fallacies. I would immerse myself in books about critical thinking and later neuroplasticity, hoping to help other people who wanted a better life. But most importantly, I would practice using my intuition and listening to my conscience.

* * *

Following those experiences, I struggled with agnosticism. Eventually, I felt the need to believe in *something*. I evaluated my options. Buddhism, New Age, Judaism, Jesus? I decided to try God.

I talked to him, but not in a religious way. I swore a lot about people who had upset me. Surprisingly, the venting made me feel closer to God. After a while, I cleaned up my language and shared deep truths about myself.

I began going into empty churches. Then full churches. But the strongest connection to God came when I walked in nature and silently talked to him. I focused on the trees, sky, mud, and flowers. I associated the beauty and ruggedness with God's goodness, kindness, and strength. Feeling gratitude toward God was healing. These walks and gratitude talks helped to clear my mind of regrets and disappointments. Having compassion for myself reduced anxiety and must have strengthened my anterior cingulate cortex.

Also, praying while walking and looking at the sky gave me a sense of awe and comfort, likely activating the periaqueductal gray area, a brain region that releases biochemicals for pain reduction and is related to altruistic behavior.[2]

Soon, these walks became a habit and a life changer. On one of them, I chose to follow the *teachings* of Jesus – such as love, forgiveness, kindness, persistence, generosity, self-control, humility, and truth.

My decision created a new problem and a big question about group thinking. A well-known television evangelist was in the news at that time. After a multitude of believers supported his blatantly lavish lifestyle, the pastor was convicted of fraud and conspiracy.

There was a warning sign in my brain. Was this another example of group dynamics gone awry? Did strong emotions – or passion for a cause – subdue reasoning, dull intuition, influence decisions, or silence insiders?

I was concerned. Could my new trust in God be misused by someone who was manipulative, dishonest, or did not share my values? How could someone or some ideology thwart my perception of lies or truths?

I had an answer. I would try to stay aware of those thinking traps and clever distractions that I had ignored in the past. And I would take time to talk with God each day. I felt supported when I found a directive in the Bible – love God with your heart, soul, *mind*, and body. To me, the directive meant God wants people to think.

Sometimes in churches I heard messages that didn't always make sense to me. The wrathful scriptures made me feel anxious or angry. Various pastors had various answers to my questions. I was confused and frustrated. When I explained to one pastor that I didn't agree with his answer, he told me to ask God. Hmmm. I liked that. I would ask. And I would talk to God about my feelings.

Through reflection and research, I eventually found meaningful answers to some of my questions. I realized that many traditions, theories, and doctrines have evolved through the centuries, resulting in different denominations and faith practices. But the core principles of scriptures are unchanging: Love God and love your neighbor as you love yourself. In other words, be fair, be merciful, and walk humbly with God.

These days, I'm more aware when people belittle reasoning or distort information. I *strive* to bless them with truth. Blessing people helps me have integrity and clarity yet feel compassion and forgiveness. Plus, those blessings inspire hope, humility, and action.

* * *

Many years later, I learned an elegant lesson about truth and humility from a woman who had been a migrant farm worker. Her son Joel Ramirez was graduating from medical school at UCLA. I introduced myself as a reporter doing a story about learning and neuroscience for the *Los Angeles Times*.

Mrs. Ramirez tilted her head and raised her hand to stop me from speaking. In accented English, she said, "Excuse me, what is neuroscience?"

I was surprised by her question, and I gave her the answer.

After the interview, I kept mulling over what happened. First, I felt bad about speaking quickly and unintentionally using a word she may not have understood.

Second, there were TV cameras and lots of media people near us on the campus. Having limited English, she could have felt intimidated or uncomfortable. But she appeared to have enough self-assurance, humility, or honesty to stop me and ask for clarification.

Mrs. Ramirez said she always wanted to be a teacher.

That day, she was mine. She was an example of integrity and dignity.

* * *

Years later while I was teaching some college courses in Oregon, I had an issue with a student. After she spoke with the dean about the problem behavior, she was allowed to return to class. I wondered how she would act and how the other students would respond to her.

On the first day when she walked back into the room, she smiled, stretched out her arms, and loudly said, "IT'S A NEW DAY!"

This student would become an example for moving forward after a mistake. I would sometimes remember her confidence when I thought of my greatest mistakes and when I faced opportunities for a new day, a better life.

Chapter 4: Truth vs. Deception

Related Science

Emotions can be transferred to other people and spread through social groups. However, some people are more susceptible than others to contagious emotion and messages, according to a 2007 study led by Remus Ilies and published in the *Journal of Applied Psychology*. The study was titled "Explaining affective linkages in teams: Individual differences in susceptibility to contagion and individualism–collectivism."

* * *

Research can help to understand the power of social relationships to make the best of a difficult situation. Psychologists studied people who lived in the slums of Calcutta and found that strong social relationships were credited with satisfaction in some life areas. The 2001 study was led by Robert Biswas-Diener and published in *Social Indicators Research*. The study was titled "Making the Best of a Bad Situation: Satisfaction in the Slums of Calcutta."

* * *

Research showed that regretting life choices can motivate goal setting. Women who made life changes based on their new goals reported having more well-being than those who did not. The 1999 study was led by Abigail J. Stewart and published in the *Journal of Personality and Social Psychology*. "If I had it to do over again…: Midlife review, midcourse corrections, and women's well-being in midlife."

Chapter 4: Truth vs. Deception

Supplementary Section

Find and Fix Thinking Traps

This special section is provided to help people identify thinking traps. We've all used them at some time or another. But as you've just read in this chapter, thinking traps can be subtle, deceptive, or blatant. They can create big problems, especially when people use them to build power and influence our opinions. Wisely, we can use the remedies below to avoid manipulation, group pressure, and herd behavior.

EMOTIONAL APPEALS: Using guilt, shame, fear, anger, or pity to motivate people to think or do something. **Remedy:** Evaluate your strong emotions.

DISTRACTION: Talking about something unrelated to switch attention from a problem. **Remedy:** Stay focused on the issue.

FALSE AUTHORITY: Using misleading statistics or statements from qualified or unqualified authorities. **Remedy:** Analyze the facts, the evidence, and the sources.

ABSOLUTE WORDS: Creating false statements by using words such as *always, never, every, only, all, none,* or *must.* **Remedy:** Listen and read carefully.

FALSE CAUSES AND EFFECTS: Excusing an action and making it sound reasonable. **Remedy:** Question excuses.

MISLEADING COMPARISONS: Comparing two situations that are not related. **Remedy:** Question possible unrelated comparisons.

LOADED QUESTIONS AND STATEMENTS: Hiding an opinion in questions, statements, or sarcasm. **Remedy:** Listen unemotionally and read carefully.

BLACK-AND-WHITE THINKING: Stating that there are only two solutions or alternatives. **Remedy:** Think about alternatives and other solutions.

ARGUING IN CIRCLES: Giving an opinion and slightly disguising the same opinion in the same sentence or argument. **Remedy:** Ask for specific details or facts.

OVER-GENERALIZATION: Making a conclusion from a few facts. **Remedy:** Ask specific questions.

BANDWAGON: Using popularity, peer pressure, and social media to make important decisions. **Remedy:** Evaluate the facts. Think for yourself.

Summary:

Listen and read carefully. Ask questions. Request specific answers.

Check assumptions. Question excuses. Get facts before making a judgment.

Use reason to balance high emotions. Analyze the evidence. Question alternatives. Think for yourself.

Groupthink Symptoms and Remedies

Most likely, we've all been in situations where some type of group thinking has occurred – work situations, social settings, and even in close relationships. The consequences may be minor, or disastrous. In the book, *Wiser: Getting Beyond Groupthink to Make Groups Wiser,* authors Cass R. Sunstein and Reid Hastie, provide ways to identify and prevent group thinking.

Symptoms:

Withholding important knowledge or opinions.

Overestimating power, expertise, credentials, or immunity.

Fearing criticism, pressure, or punishment.

Labeling questions or opposing opinions as weak or bad.

Requiring uniform thinking.

Mistaking silence as agreement or unity.

Increasing extremism.

Remedies:

Encourage and support people who listen, inquire, and evaluate.

Request diverse opinions.

Challenge thinking traps or logical fallacies.

Get outside opinions or support if necessary.

Maintain your values and virtues. Stay safe.

Evaluate News Reports

We are bombarded by news reports and social media that can influence our judgement and decision making. However, asking questions can help prevent deception and increase our critical thinking skills. To evaluate information and save time and money, you may want to use these helpful questions adapted from *The Art and Craft of Feature Writing: Based on the Wall Street Journal Guide,* by William Blundell.

BACKGROUND: Who or what is the source of this information? Is this source reliable? Is the information first-hand or second-hand? Are these facts or opinions?

SIZE: What's the importance or meaning of this event or new situation? How many people, places, or things are affected?

REASONS: Why is this news happening now? Is it money, politics, law, health, religion, emotions, or relationships? What are the values or beliefs of the people in the news? How are they typical or unique?

IMPACT: Who is being hurt? Who is being helped? How does this news affect finance, politics, emotions, health, religion, or other factors?

COUNTERACTION: Who or what organizations are working for this or against this news?

FUTURE: What do experts say? What do non-experts say? What are their hopes, plans, or goals for the future?

Dear Reader,

Each journey involves roads on which we walk gracefully or stumble – sometimes painfully.

Unaware, we may be misdirected.

Without maps, we look for strangers to join forces.

We may get lost.

Together, we let go of failure or shame.

Alone, we cling to self-forgiveness, to self-compassion.

All searching, we find our way to Hope.

Rosie

Chapter 4: Truth vs. Deception

Inspiration and Affirmations

The Lord is near to all who call on him, to all who call on him in truth. Psalms 145:18 (ESV)

Affirmations: I talk to God when I feel overwhelmed or confused by challenging events, information, or emotions. I remember that God is near me, and he can help.

Write your own affirmations:

_____

_____

_____

You will know the truth, and the truth will set you free. John 8:32 (ESV)

Affirmations: I know that speaking the truth can free me of burdens. But even if I can't tell the truth to someone, I can tell God the truth.

Write your own affirmations:

_____

_____

_____

Teach me your way, O Lord, that I may walk in your truth. Psalm 86:11 (ESV)

Affirmations: I will be honest with myself and others.

Write your own affirmations:

_____

_____

_____

Let us not love in word or talk, but in deed and in truth. 1 John 3:18 (ESV)

Affirmations: I can and will act lovingly.

Write your own affirmations:

_____

_____

_____

Love forgets mistakes. Proverbs 17:9 (TLB)

Affirmations: I love myself, so I can learn from my mistakes. I refuse to berate and hurt myself about my errors.

Write your own affirmations:

_____

_____

_____

Be gentle and ready to forgive; never hold grudges. Remember, the Lord forgives you, so you must forgive others. Colossians 3:13 (TLB)

Affirmations: I forgive myself, and I'm grateful that God removes guilt and shame. He forgives me, and his forgiveness helps me to forgive people who hurt me.

Write your own affirmations:

_____

_____

_____

Chapter 5

Persistence vs. Quitting

Like many moms of her era, my mom had a favorite saying, "If at first you don't succeed, try, try again."

Divorced, she raised five girls, including a set of twins and a daughter with brain damage. She worked in a drycleaner, volunteered for civil rights projects, and taught us about the Holocaust. She earned her high-school equivalency certificate in her late 30s, and finally got a driver's license in her 40s. I know other people have had greater challenges. Still, she had a big workload.

When I was a teenager, she was quickly preparing the upper level of our two-story house to be a rental. She asked me and my 10-year-old sister to help her move a refrigerator up a flight of stairs.

"We can't do it, Ma. We gotta get some guys to help."

When necessary, she would flag down guys walking on our street and pay them a few dollars to help with heavy work. This was the 1960s.

"There aren't any guys around. We have to do it today!" she said. She needed the money. So, we struggled with the refrigerator.

When we were near the top of the stairs, the refrigerator got stuck.

"We CAN'T do this, Mom!

She yelled like a wild woman, *"I CAN do this!"* And with a bolt of energy, she shoved. It moved! She forced it up the stairs!

My mom was raised in a coal-mining town, and she had a habit that embarrassed me: She prayed out loud. Some people mockingly called her "Holy Mary." But that afternoon, she had been swearing a lot in Serbian. She probably used all her resources – grit and God. In this case, adrenaline was definitely pumping!

An interesting point: research has shown that swearing can reduce pain perception and increase heart rate in some people.[1]

* * *

In unusual ways, my mom demanded persistence from us.

When I was 19, a friend was driving me home one night and another driver ran a red light. He hit my side of the car, and my head slammed onto the dashboard. The result was a concussion and partial amnesia.

The police drove me home. I didn't know the date or year. Memories of people and places were scrambled or non-existent. When my sisters saw me, they were terrified.

"Do you remember me?"

"Rosie, what's my name?"

My mom was tired and angry.

"What were you smoking?"

"Nothing!"

"What were you drinking?"

"Nothing!"

The police drove us to the hospital.

After several hours, I was released from the emergency room, and I expected my mom to call a cab.

"We're walking."

"But it's late at night! And it's freezing outside."

As we trudged along darkened streets, I tried to remember details of my life.

I'd ask her, "Is that right?"

"Wrong. Try again."

I tried to remember where I worked.

"Wrong. Try again."

When we got home, it seemed like my mom stayed awake with me for hours while I drank tea and ate buttered saltines and tried to remember. I think she still had to go to work in the morning.

Five days later, I was able to recall which buses would take me to my job. But I'm not sure how productive I was when I arrived. After a couple of weeks, I seemed to have all my wits together.

I sometimes attribute my fast recovery to my mom's persistence and the adrenaline produced by her bluntness.[2] Maybe she hoped that walking in freezing temperatures would sharpen my awareness. Or maybe the prospect of having another daughter with a brain problem had triggered every fear and anxiety circuit in *her* brain.

For someone who boldly trusted God, my mom must have been tapping into some deep survival wisdom.

* * *

Two decades after that car accident in Detroit, my mom and sister Patty moved to California. Patty lived in a nursing home about an hour from my mom's house. My mom wouldn't drive on the Los Angeles freeways, so my sisters and I would take her to see Patty.

Although my mom visited Patty a couple of times each week, she was determined to see her more often.

She began taking buses to the nursing home. The trip lasted a few hours. We were concerned about her, but when we learned more, we were shocked.

In the early evenings, she would transfer buses and wait alone on a street near Skid Row in downtown L.A.

"Mom!! Please, it's not safe!!!"

With absolute confidence, she said, "I am praying, and I know that my God is with me! I *will* be safe!"

Pleading and arguing was useless. She was trusting God. And she persisted. Safely.

* * *

My mom *loved* the weather and foliage in Southern California, especially after living in Detroit for decades. California would become her home for more than 25 years. After an illness, she went on hospice for a year. But the following year her condition improved, and she proudly "graduated."

I visited my mom on a beautiful summer day when she was in a small nursing home. She wanted to walk outside and smell the flowers, but the nurse explained that her muscles were too weak for her to walk. We could take her out in a wheelchair. The nurse and I left the room to talk about my mom's condition.

A few minutes later, we heard a loud thud. Running back into the room, we saw my mom slumped on the floor. Looking like a defiant kid who got caught smoking a cigarette, she smirked, "I *like* taking risks!"

* * *

Just before entering high school, I took drum lessons and then a long-term prayer was answered. By learning to read music, I overcame a speech impediment. Like my mom and sister, I stuttered in stressful situations. When I felt like I was going to stumble on words or phrases, I'd imagine seeing a rest note in sheet music. I'd take a breath to disrupt the timing of my speech. Sometimes when I spoke, I'd think of jazz rhythms or accent marks on music notes. By changing my breathing and timing patterns, I could speak normally.

I understand that stuttering is linked to reduced blood flow in the Broca's area of the brain, and I know that stuttering sometimes stops at the time of puberty.[3] But I think praying for years about the problem helped to boost my resilience and kept me looking for ways to fix the speech problem.

During my teen years in Detroit, I had planned for a career in music, either playing on stage or in recording sessions. One night, scouts watched our band perform, and our lead singer got a contract with Motown Records.

But other changes were in store for me. My music career gradually ended because repeatedly using the kick drum caused severe pain in an already problematic knee.

On the upbeat, I would eventually get connected with Motown in L.A. – working happily at a desk job in their royalties department.

* * *

A few months before graduating from high school, a teacher gave me a suggestion: Go to college. I never thought that was possible! I quickly applied to Wayne State University, got accepted, and received a grant for low-income students. But I didn't have study skills. After a year, I quit school. Often, nightmares of my failure and lost opportunities haunted me.

When I was 30, I shifted away from agnosticism and tip-toed toward faith. I began to ask God for help, and I found a way to read difficult information. If my eyes drifted, or I was confused, I'd point to the words, pause briefly, and picture their meaning. Then I could understand what I was reading.

This new ability inspired the hope that I could have a meaningful career. I read the book *What Color Is Your Parachute?* and learned I had the qualities of a writer and teacher – even though I didn't have the skills. But the author wrote that skills could be learned. So, I studied grammar books for third graders, writing books for teens, and college textbooks for future journalists.

* * *

In 1990, I was trying to resolve a big problem, and I needed some inspiration. Black gospel music had given me hope in the past, and I heard that Grammy award-winning singer Andrae Crouch would have a concert soon in a church in Pacoima, near Los Angeles. I gathered some friends, and we went to see him.

Sitting in the Black church and waiting for the concert to start, I couldn't help but remember being a kid in Detroit and hiding with my sister outside a storefront church in our neighborhood. We loved the music – so rich, so powerful, and so different from what we were hearing during the Latin masses in our Catholic church.

My experience in Pacoima reached a new level of surprise when the singers and musicians walked onto the stage. They were all blonde and white! What was going on?!

I learned Andrae Crouch had visited Norway and worked with the Oslo Gospel Choir. Now they were in Pacoima to perform with Crouch and promote their new album.

The contrasting experiences were exactly what I'd been reading about in my journalism textbooks. This was a newsworthy story. *This* was my chance.

During the concert, everyone was standing and clapping or dancing by their seats. The feeling was electric. The first chance I got, I fumbled through my purse to find paper and began taking notes. But I was out of sync with the rest of the group, and my friend nudged me to stop writing. I did. For a minute. And then I thought, if I don't do this, I'm going to be *really* depressed. So, I pulled out my scrap paper again and took notes about everything around me, just like I'd learned to do from my textbooks.

The next morning, I was reeling with energy. What happened? Why did the singing, music, and movement have such a profound effect on me? And what magazine would publish this amazing news?

71

I prayed sincerely. Then I flipped open a book on my shelf, *The Religious Writers Marketing Guide,* and saw a listing for *Contemporary Christian Music* magazine. I drafted a pitch letter and made the phone call. Yes, they were interested in the story, but only if I had photos. I didn't.

Yet, I recalled seeing someone taking pictures at the concert and called the church. Finally, I got connected to the man and his photos. I did the interviews with Andrae Crouch and the Norwegian choir director, wrote the story, and the article ran. It would be the start of my writing career.

* * *

About a month later, Andrae Crouch called me to attend a memorial service for the gospel music legend James Cleveland. Stevie Wonder, Aretha Franklin, Gladys Knight, and other performers who had been inspired by Cleveland would be there.

I'd been advised by a *real* journalist to stay out of a press pool if I saw one forming. But the press coordinator knew I had written for a Christian magazine, and she pulled me into the swarm of reporters so I could interview Stevie Wonder. He talked about the importance of gospel music. Afterward, she walked me toward the dressing rooms, put her hand on a door, and said, "You have 30 seconds."

I asked Gladys Knight the question that had been on my mind since the concert in Los Angeles, "What makes gospel music so powerful?" To my surprise, she sadly shook her head and said that people don't really understand gospel music. And she ended the interview.

I knew that spirituals and sacred songs were a catalyst for courage and the emancipation of slaves. Gospel music reflected the experiences of Blacks when they were free. The music included worship songs that continued to inspire faith and hope. But something else was happening with the music.

My question would be answered 20 years later when I interviewed the author of *"This is Your Brain on Music,"* neuroscientist and cognitive psychologist David Levitin.

"Gospel music reinforces the neural pathways associated with positive thinking and positive outcomes," said Levitin. "It distracts people when they're feeling blue and rewires the brain to accommodate positive biochemicals. That changes the structure and function of the brain."

Also, people who sing together experience the release of feel-good hormones – oxytocin, prolactin, and dopamine – and the effects of those chemicals can linger. It's not sufficient to simply sing, you have to be engaged and make the experience meaningful, Levitin said. An exhilarating emotion or experience can alter the neuro-configuration of the brain, but boring experiences might not.

Clapping, moving, or dancing are important. "When you're moving, you have more neurons firing and involved, and that makes the activity more memorable. So, the emotion will be better recalled," Levitin said. He was alluding to Hebb's rule: Neurons that fire together – wire together.[4,5]

Levitin added, "If you want to change the brain reliably, you don't do something once, you engage it on a regular basis."

After 20 years, I finally had an answer to a question I knew was important. Yet the greatest importance of gospel music and spirituals has been known for centuries by those who suffered horribly and used faith and music for hope and survival.

* * *

By my mid-40s, I was a divorced mom, and I *really* needed to earn money. Writing freelance articles for the *San Bernardino Sun* didn't provide enough income. So, I wrote ads and voiced radio commercials for a couple of years. Later, I found a temporary but high paying assignment that would require quitting my current job at a radio station. I took the risk.

The assignment with Loma Linda University Medical Center was beyond my scope. I was definitely out of my league. I would be interviewing international nutrition experts and Walter Willett from Harvard. The editor had confidence in me, but when I finally received the preparatory background material, I panicked. The science research was dense and detailed.

As I drove to Loma Linda, I repeated an encouraging sentence from the Bible for the two-hour drive. When I arrived, I felt calm and confident. I really *believed* what I'd been saying, "I can do all things through Christ who strengthens me." Plus, I felt peaceful, thinking that God was with me.

Within a couple of months, I would sign a contract to write a weekly health and nutrition column for the university and distribute it to newspapers around the country. Reducing stress and understanding science became much easier on the days when I relied on God. That meant talking to him.

"So, Lord, what do you think I should do here?"

I would take several deep breaths to relax. Then I'd write my concerns and list the possible solutions. I never heard an audible voice that told me what to do.

I'd hear my inner voice – intuition, conscience, memory, reasoning, or random thoughts.[6,7] Were the out-of-the-blue thoughts inspired by God, or were they a part of normal mental functions?

Science can't answer that question. Nevertheless, I believe healthy brain functioning and a sense of moral law (knowledge of right and wrong) can contribute to the perception of guidance. I believe the combination is a gift from God.

Often, I'd get a great idea, and I'd thank God. Other times, I'd make the most logical choice, and I'd thank God. In any case, I would feel peaceful talking to God who I perceived as loving and helpful. Then the anxiety and fuzzy thinking would be replaced with better decision making. When I briefly talked to God throughout the day, my work would be better. At this time, my faith was quickly growing. I had been part of a weekly prayer group led by a Jamaican woman and her husband from Ghana. There, I heard faith-filled prayers of people from Congo, India, the U.S., and other countries.

* * *

To meet other writers, I organized a small group of journalists who were Christians and wrote for the *Los Angeles Times* and the *Chicago Tribune*. They encouraged me to write for the *L.A. Times*. So, I started by pitching and selling stories about what I knew and liked most – drums and music.

While interviewing people, I learned to trust my gut feelings. When I didn't trust my intuition, inevitably my editor would send me back to the source for more information, which would cost me time and money. Journalism was helping me develop the critical thinking skills that had been thwarted at other times in my life.

In addition, staying in touch with God and following my intuition was leading me to important sources and providing more opportunities to write for the *Times* about business and other topics.

Plus, my reporting skills increased my ability to take better notes during sermons and to carefully read and paraphrase scriptures.

With the encouragement of other reporters, I finally signed up for an algebra class I'd been avoiding since high school. I accepted that I had a problem with math anxiety, so I read books about it, and finally found a way to feel better.

I'd dance around the house and say, *"I love math. This is going to be great!"* Of course, I was pretending. I felt weird doing it and ended up laughing at myself. But my confidence increased, and I was feeling ready for the challenge.

By this time, I understood that my affirmations were decreasing activity in my amygdala and boosting activity in the brain circuits associated with hope and motivation. Also, exercise (dancing) helped to increase attention by stimulating nerve cells in the hippocampus.[8]

* * *

Because understanding math concepts had been difficult for me, I took some tests to assess my learning abilities. When I finished, the test administrator brought the program director into the room. They looked concerned.

"Are you partially blind?"

"What?! "No, I'm not."

I'd scored well on the language and reading portions of the test, but I failed the visual section. Although my first five answers were correct, I didn't have sufficient time to answer the next 25 questions.

Additional testing was offered to me, but I was so discouraged and ashamed of myself that I didn't continue testing. However later, I created helpful exercises that improved my ability to translate images into words.

As I learned more about neuroscience and study strategies, my college courses became easier. A few years later at age 61, I was utterly grateful to God when I finally graduated – magna cum laude.

I knew other people faced similar learning challenges, and I wanted to help them. In Boston, I had the opportunity to share what I'd learned with low-income women between the ages of 16 and 60 who had experienced trauma. To help them pass their high school equivalency tests, I taught writing skills, study strategies, and reading comprehension.

I would always stop teaching my class on the days when a student walked into the room beaming with pride because she just received news that she passed all the required exams. Then *she* would become the teacher for that hour. She was the role model and the representative for hope.

Later during the graduation ceremonies, it was breathtaking to see persistent women who finally reached their goals.

* * *

Sometimes when I feel good, I find myself taking all the credit for these accomplishments – overcoming a speech impediment, learning how to learn and think critically, having a meaningful career, finally earning my degree, and then teaching others.

Sometimes I forget the gritty persistence of my parents who, in their own ways, used faith *and adrenaline* to overcome hardships and survive.

And sometimes, when I take the time to remember the depth and duration of God's daily help, the whole picture of growth looks very different. I wasn't alone. I had the Source of Hope near me. And when I chose to connect, I experienced his power.

Chapter 5: Persistence vs. Quitting

Related Science

Students can learn to persist in environments that foster growth and teach grit. Authors Aaron Hochanadel and Dora Finamore provide suggestions for increasing grit and persistence in students. The 2015 paper was published in the *Journal of International Education Research* and titled "Fixed and growth mindset in education and how grit helps students persist in the face of adversity."

* * *

Doing activities related to long-term goals produced activity in the prefrontal cortex and released good-feeling dopamine in the nucleus accumbens. The 2005 study was led by Yukiori Goto and published in *Nature Neuroscience.* The study was titled "Dopaminergic modulation of limbic and cortical drive of nucleus accumbens in goal-directed behavior."

* * *

Dopamine levels help to regulate motivation to do positive activities. But for some people who are sensation seekers, dopamine can regulate motivation to do negative activities. The 2012 study led by John D. Salamone was published in *Neuron.* The study is titled "The mysterious motivational functions of mesolimbic dopamine."

Chapter 5: Persistence vs. Quitting

Supplementary Section

Learn for Success

I *love* sharing shortcuts to help people learn faster and achieve their goals. Using these suggestions can engage several brain areas and make it easier to read and remember important points. If you know someone who might benefit from these tips, please consider sharing them.

The **PAGES** method below was adapted from the book, *Student Success Secrets* by Eric Jensen.

Preview: Start with affirmations to increase self-confidence. Read the title, headings, subheadings, or bold words. Read photo captions.

Ask Questions: What is this about? What do I already know? What could be important to me?

Get key words: Find words that seem important. Circle them. Or on Word documents, mark key words with bold font. Look up definitions for new words. For difficult information, try this: Point as you read. Pause often. Picture what the words mean. When you understand the difficult section, continue reading normally.

Explain with emotion: At the end of a paragraph, page, or chapter, say what you've just read. Use your own words. *Emphasize* some words to create emotion. Connect the new information to what you already know.

Select: Pick important points to remember. Write them down. Outline them or draw pictures.

Energy for Learning

Reading or studying can be tiring sometimes because it requires self-control to concentrate. The energy to maintain self-control comes from glucose, and it can be depleted quickly when we're studying. To get more glucose in your bloodstream, try these suggestions:

Exhale and inhale slowly and deeply for a few minutes.

Express positive affirmations.

Exercise or stretch.

Eat a small healthy snack. Better yet, drink lots of water.

Also, separate big tasks into small tasks, so you'll get a sense of accomplishment more often. (Thanks to dopamine.) Try working in segments of 45-60 minutes, then take a brief break to stay alert and function at your best level.

Improve Your Memory

Here are some tricks to recalling information.

Review new information shortly after you read it or hear it. *Don't* strive to recall information *exactly* as it was first learned. Just start talking or writing notes, and then the neural pathways for the memories will become engaged. The more you write or say the little bits of information, the more likely memories will be recalled.

Reread your notes within 24 hours after a lesson or lecture.

Recall the information in a few days and then in a week. If it's important, review it again in a few weeks. Otherwise, memories may fade.

De-Stress to Learn Faster

When we're trying to learn something and we feel stressed or depressed, then concentrating may be more difficult. That's because certain brain chemicals can prevent some electrical impulses from quickly moving across the spaces between brain cells. It may be difficult to remember or learn about information that doesn't relate to *survival*.

But we can do things to reduce stress and learn more. Exercising, deep breathing, meditating, praying, or frequently saying positive affirmations can help us. Then we can learn faster. We can remember more. We can think creatively.

This explains why it's important to take brief breaks to breathe or pray when we're studying, concentrating, or making big decisions.

Big tip: As we age, we may not have the same intellectual demands that we had in earlier years. Still, it's important to keep reading, learning, and talking (or writing) about what we've learned. The process sharpens memory and critical thinking. Life-long learning also improves our ability to make good decisions and maintain a healthy lifestyle.

Important: If you're having a difficult time learning something, engage more of your senses. In other words: See it. Say it. Hear it. Write it. Move it. You'll get it!

Dear Reader,

For those of us who have been arrested by fear or failure, here is my version of the Miranda Rights.

> *"You have the right to remain hopeful and persistent.*
>
> *Anything positive you say can and will be used for you in the court of life.*
>
> *You have the right to refuse despair, procrastination, and revenge.*
>
> *You have the right to contact your Creator.*
>
> *If you cannot afford the time to speak with your Creator, additional life lessons may be provided for you.*
>
> *Do you understand the rights I have written for you?"*

Rosie

Chapter 5: Persistence vs. Quitting

Inspiration and Affirmations

Be bold and strong! Banish fear and doubt! For remember, the Lord your God is with you wherever you go." Joshua 1:9 (TLB)

Affirmations: I am strong and courageous. I refuse to be anxious about my work. I can remember that God is with me.

Write your own affirmations:

_____

_____

_____

Fight the good fight of faith. 1 Timothy 6:12 (NIV)

Affirmations: I imagine overcoming the obstacles that I will face today. I will choose to fight fear with faith.

Write your own affirmations:

_____

_____

_____

Let us not become weary in doing good, for at the proper time we will reap a harvest if we do not give up. Galatians 6:9 (NIV)

Affirmations: I refuse to quit. I rest when I'm tired, but I won't give up! I believe that there will be a payoff for my hard work and for doing the right things.

Write your own affirmations:

_____

_____

_____

Since we are surrounded by such a great cloud of witnesses, let us throw off everything that hinders and the sin that so easily entangles, and let us run with perseverance the race marked out for us. Hebrews 12:1 (NIV)

Affirmations: I envision persisting and achieving my purpose in life. I can ignore distractions and things that throw me off my course.

Write your own affirmations:

_____

_____

_____

I can do all things through him who gives me strength. Philippians 4:12 (NIV)

Affirmations: I *can* do all things through Christ who strengthens me. I imagine getting help from God and completing my goals.

Write your own affirmations:

_____

_____

_____

Chapter 6

Courage vs. Fear

I had always thought that when I had grandchildren, I would want to live near them. But when I was working on my bachelor's degree as a 59-year-old in California, it wasn't my plan to move to Oregon. That's where my pregnant daughter and her husband were working on their degrees.

My daughter had severe migraines since she was four years old, and I believed the headaches and pregnancy would challenge her efforts to obtain her degree. I knew the importance of having an education, and I didn't want my daughter or her family to experience struggles like mine.

Still, I had conflicting feelings. I was sad thinking about leaving family, friends, and my home in California. And then renting a bedroom in someone else's house to save money. But I was thrilled that I could graduate sooner at a university in Oregon, and I was propelled by the lure of the new baby.

My wise pastor from Brazil gave me a suggestion that was pivotal: Find scripture verses relating to courage and repeat them often. Then don't look back.

* * *

After three years in Oregon, there were three graduations: my son-in-law's, my daughter's, and mine. As my daughter walked across the stage to receive her diploma, she carried her second baby.

The following year, I would need to make another decision. Would I accept their invitation to move again – this time, to Boston where my son-in-law was accepted to graduate school?

Oh, that was easy. No way!!

I was now in a program for a master's degree in neuropsychology, and I worked as a research assistant in a brain electrophysiology lab. Plus, I taught part-time at a community college, and I did freelance writing for a medical center.

Leave Oregon? You're kidding, right?!

But the nagging thought of leaving my two grandkids made me sad. And I imagined the challenges of my daughter and son-in-law as he tried to complete a graduate program with a baby and a preschooler. All that and more kept me thinking. And praying. And remembering God's help in the past.

So, I thought: What was my purpose in life anyway? I was drawn to altruism, maybe for selfish reasons – such as the feelings of love.

While I was considering my options, it seemed crucial to focus more on God. For weeks, I took prayer walks, talked to him, and repeated those courage-boosting scriptures. I needed time alone to think and pray. Then I decided. I would go.

Many nights after making my decision, I would listen to one hymn over and over again: *Be Thou My Vision*. The lyrics and Irish drum rhythms built my courage. I needed God to lead me in a new city where I didn't know anyone and where I didn't have a job.

The transition would involve two tasks. Rent a room for myself and help to find a house for my daughter's family – they would be arriving two months later.

It would be tricky to find a room in Boston where a housing crisis existed. So, I carefully crafted an email and sent it to 23 churches. A couple of days later, I found a place – subletting from two teachers for the summer. More gratitude. More confidence.

After I sold all my furniture and stuffed my car with clothes, I said goodbye to friends and loved ones. I would meet my daughter and her family in Boston after summer school classes ended.

My sister Dolores joined me to drive eastward, stopping in Michigan to visit another sister. After that, I'd be traveling alone. Still, I knew God would be with me.

While I was on the road to Boston, high anxiety about not having a job was buffered when I thanked God *in advance* for what I believed he would do for me. As I approached the Massachusetts state line, I received a call from a former client. He said he had just emailed a new contract and would be sending me a retainer check as soon as I gave him my new address.

Thank you, Lord!

The news must have triggered the reward system in my brain. Undoubtedly, there would be more prayers and more trust in God.

* * *

Finding an affordable rental for my daughter's family was the next big challenge. As the arrival date for my daughter's family approached, I was worried. My subletting arrangement would end soon, and I hadn't found anything for my daughter's family, even though we had contacted *many* landlords and real estate agents. The final total would be 350.

When I couldn't sleep and felt panicky, I'd get out of bed and do something that a physician mentioned when I interviewed her for the *Los Angeles Times* article, *"Too stressed to Learn."*[1]

Raised in poverty, Shauna Blake Collins, M.D. fought fear during nearly 14 years of education. A dropout from a South-Central Los Angeles high school, she earned a GED diploma at 22, became a licensed vocational nurse, then a registered nurse, and finally, at 41, she became a physician.

In medical school, Collins often struggled and would lie awake at night for hours with her books open, feeling paralyzed by anxiety and unable to study.

After she heard a sermon about getting rid of fear, everything changed. She did something that could seem strange. When she was very anxious, she would get out of bed, walk around her living room and pray. She would "take authority" over her negative thoughts. She would firmly "tell" the negative thoughts to stop. Then she would repeat encouraging affirmations or scripture verses. Finally, she'd spend time thanking God.

It's easy to understand the idea of affirmations and gratitude. But the idea of audibly and firmly telling negative thoughts to stop can seem embarrassing and weird. Yet there is something compelling about the idea of being bold, or even angry, to increase motivation. The process is similar to what some people might do to psych themselves up for a sports competition. Could anger motivate *some* people to function or perform better? That was a question asked by researchers who studied combat capabilities.[2] And the answer was yes.

Anyway, I copied Dr. Blake. After about 45 minutes, I'd usually feel sleepy and go back to bed. I figured that moving around and praying released stress. It took a lot less time than staying in bed and worrying all night. Plus, I felt closer to God and more hopeful.

Some nights when the psych-myself-up approach didn't work, I'd lay in bed and whisper kindly to myself, as I would a little child. I needed to *hear* nurturing words to offset worried thoughts. I'm sure self-compassion and trust in God helped to decrease stress chemicals and increase oxytocin.

Soon, I got a tip from a realtor. She bluntly told me to quit trying to find an apartment for my daughter's family. "Instead, find a house for yourself *and* your whole family in an outlying area and sign the lease."

Although we were uneasy about the proposed living arrangement, everyone agreed to adapt.

Next, I decided to follow another woman's advice, and I finally checked the online bulletin boards at churches. There was an ad for a beautiful three-story townhouse with a separate living area on the lower level, *and* a pond near the gardens. When I phoned the woman, she asked, "What took you so long to call? The ad was up there for ten days."

The lease was signed, and my daughter's whole family arrived in Boston ten days before the new school term began.

Thank you, Power of my power!

Chapter 6: Courage vs. Fear

Related Science

When a person makes an *effort* to overcome the fear of something, this effort causes activity in the brain region called the subgenual anterior cingulate cortex. It's believed that the subgenual anterior cingulate cortex reduces the response to fear in other areas of the brain so that the person can act with courage. The 2010 study was led by Uri Nili and published in *Neuron*. The study was titled "Fear Thou Not: Activity of Frontal and Temporal Circuits in Moments of Real-Life Courage."

* * *

Acute or chronic stress or anxiety can reduce the ability to solve problems and think creatively. In an experiment with 80 undergraduates, those who used self-affirmations showed an improvement in their problem-solving abilities. The 2013 study was led by J. David Creswell and published in *PLOS ONE*. The study was titled "Self-affirmation improves problem-solving under stress."

* * *

Researchers analyzed two long-term studies and found that when people experienced a life transition, gratitude protected them from depression and anxiety. Also, gratitude promoted social support. The 2008 study was led by Alex M. Wood and published in the *Journal of Research in Personality*. The study was titled "The role of gratitude in the development of social support, stress, and depression: Two longitudinal studies."

Dear Reader,

We start each journey with challenges, known and unknown.

Hope propels us.

We take bold steps.

Sometimes, fear-filled steps.

Our Power guides us.

Courage fills us.

Resilience follows us.

Our Power welcomes us.

Rosie

Chapter 6: Courage vs. Fear

Inspiration and Affirmations

This is my command—be strong and courageous! Do not be afraid or discouraged. For the Lord your God is with you wherever you go. Joshua 1:9 (NLT)

Affirmations: I am strong and courageous! God is with me.

Write your own affirmations:

_____

_____

_____

Perfect love casts out fear. 1 John 4:18 (NKJV)

Affirmations: I believe that God loves me. I speak and act lovingly to others and myself.

Write your own affirmations:

_____

_____

_____

When I am weak, then I am strong. 2 Corinthians 12:10 (NIV)

Affirmations: When I feel weak, I will imagine myself feeling strong from God's power.

Write your own affirmations:

_____

_____

_____

God has given me power, love, and self-control. 2 Timothy. 1:7 (ESV)

Affirmations: I believe God has given me the power to think clearly, act wisely, and give lovingly.

Write your own affirmations:

_____

_____

_____

Do not worry about tomorrow, for tomorrow will worry about itself. Each day has enough trouble of its own. Matthew 6:34 (NIV)

Affirmations: I trust God to help me with the obstacles I may face today. Tomorrow, he'll help me again.

Write your own affirmations:

_____

_____

_____

I will make my people strong with power from me! They will go wherever they wish, and wherever they go, they will be under my personal care. Zechariah 10:12 (TLB)

Affirmations: I can think of God's power making me strong. I can receive his personal care, so I do what I need to do and go where I need to go.

Write your own affirmations:

_____

_____

_____

Do not be anxious for anything; but in everything, by prayer and petition, with thanksgiving, present your requests to God. Philippians 4:6 (NIV)

Affirmations: I can remember to ask God for what I need today. Then I thank him, even before my prayers are answered! If I worry again, I will thank him again for his promised help.

Write your own affirmations:

_____

_____

_____

Do not be afraid or discouraged because of this vast army. For the battle is not yours, but God's. 2 Chronicles 20:15 (NIV)

Affirmations: I will be courageous. I can imagine that I am not the only one managing these challenges. God is here. I am not discouraged or paralyzed by these problems. I can pray. I can think. I can take the next right step.

Write your own affirmations:

_____

_____

_____

Let the peace of Christ rule your hearts, since as members of one body you were called to peace. Be thankful. Colossians 3:15 (NIV)

Affirmations: I picture God's peace around me and inside me. I am grateful for all his blessings – big and small.

Write your own affirmations:

_____

_____

_____

Do not fear, for I am with you; do not be dismayed, for I am your God. I will strengthen you and help you; I will uphold you with my righteous right hand. Isaiah 41:10 (NIV)

Affirmations: I trust that God is with me. I refuse to be afraid. I believe that I'll be strengthened.

Write your own affirmations:

_____

_____

_____

Chapter 7

Healing vs. Pain

I carefully re-read the question on the dental consent form: Do you have temporomandibular joint disorder (TMJ)? No. I hadn't been bothered by it in almost 20 years. So, I didn't have it anymore. Right?

After the extensive dental work was finished and the anesthetic wore off, I felt horrible. Headaches and facial pain continued for months. It was difficult to eat and sleep. I went to three different TMJ specialists in Los Angeles. X-rays and scans showed severe degeneration of the condyle bone in my jaw. I used a bite guard and followed my dentist's directions – hot-cold compresses, exercise, relaxation techniques, vitamins, supplements, anti-inflammatory foods, and a soft diet. He said there was a *slim* chance this might result in new bone growth. In the meantime, I was still in pain.

One night at 2:00 a.m. I couldn't tolerate the pain anymore and crawled out of bed. I had to talk to someone. I remembered watching a Christian TV program and seeing a phone number to call for prayer. I'd scoffed at healings by television evangelists, but now I was desperate. I found the number and called it.

As I waited to talk to someone, a recording played Bible verses. I was irritated. I didn't want to hear scriptures. More tension. More pain.

Yet instinctively, I knew I had to make a decision to believe God could help me. I started repeating the scriptures I was hearing. I forced myself to ignore my skeptical thoughts. Minutes later, a man came on the phone line.

Without any introduction or discussion, I continued praying aloud, "I believe…God can stop this pain…in my jaw…." We kept praying together.

After about twenty minutes, I realized the pain was gone. We thanked God profusely, and I got off the phone. Then I wrote down exactly what happened. I slept well for the first time in months.

The next morning, I immediately read and re-wrote my notes. I knew I needed to stop checking if the pain was coming back. And it seemed crucial to continue thanking God.

In the following weeks when the pain twinges triggered worries, I forced myself to smile and thank God again for healing me. I repeatedly spoke the Bible verses. I distracted myself and *refused* to focus on the pain. Surprisingly, this helped immensely.

Three months later, TMJ specialist Dr. David Shirazi took new images of my jaw and was shocked by what he saw. The images showed new bone growth. I was thrilled.

I don't know exactly when new growth began, but I *absolutely* know the intense pain stopped twenty minutes after I made the *choice* to believe God could heal me.

I believe that prayers had a role in my recovery. Trusting God and praying when I was in extreme pain is likely to have initiated activity in the periaqueductal gray region, an area related to spirituality and pain reduction.[1]

Maybe having hope and a positive belief system is *one* way God designed our brains and bodies to heal. There is no doubt that optimism can have a profound impact on body systems and promote health.[2] And there are unusual cases of spontaneous healing that have been verified by physicians.[3] Some people may call them miracles.

Also, people may wonder if my experience was an example of the placebo effect – which is a positive health outcome based on a person's belief that the intervention or treatment will help. It's the opposite phenomenon of the nocebo effect – which is a negative health outcome based on a person's negative beliefs.[4] Both effects are real.

I believe that God created a system for optimal health and healing, and prayer is part of that system. Even though I don't have all the answers to explain my experience, I am still supremely grateful for the new bone growth.

* * *

A few months later, I experienced trauma-related anxiety and typical prayers weren't working. A visiting minister who was well known for healing suggested something I'd never heard before.

"Pick five scriptures about overcoming fear and say them aloud three times a day. Do it for a week, and then call me if necessary."

It took time and energy to say affirmations and hopeful words three times a day while walking. But the process worked. I was on the road to feeling better.

Someone later asked me, "Were you trusting God to change circumstances or were you trusting yourself?"

Trusting God. He gave me a brain, choices, and words to use to change my circumstances and my life.

"Is this some new style of praying?"

It might be an ancient one. Early Christians and others who didn't read or write must have memorized inspiring words by repeating them and recalling them. It may have been part of a process that improved their lives.

Chapter 7: Healing vs. Pain

Related Science

A large analysis of 20 neuroimaging studies involving 600 healthy participants showed that placebo treatments affected several areas in the brain that process pain. The 2021 study was led by Mathias Zunhammer and published in *Nature Communications*. The study was titled "Meta-analysis of neural systems underlying placebo analgesia from individual participant fMRI data."

* * *

Self-affirmations can act as a shock absorber for threatening information, restoring self-confidence, and self-worth. A 2016 study found that self-affirmations cause activity in several areas of the brain including the powerful reward circuit. The research was led by Christopher N. Cascio and published in *Social Cognitive and Affective Neuroscience*. The study was titled "Self-affirmation activates brain systems associated with self-related processing and reward and is reinforced by future orientation."

* * *

Researchers found that greater proportions of African Americans and Hispanic American compared to European Americans reported using prayer for health reasons. Researchers Frank Gillum and Derek M. Griffith published the 2010 paper in the *Journal of Religion and Health*. The paper was titled "Prayer and spiritual practices for health reasons among American adults: The role of race and ethnicity."

Dear Reader,

Pain has the power to make us bitter, to make us sneer –

Or to suspend our license to scoff.

Desperation can open minds, or close minds, or expand options.

God. Reason. Instinct. Memory. Intuition. Conscience.

All used for our survival.

All the stuff of hope and faith.

Rosie

Chapter 7: Healing vs. Pain

Inspiration and Affirmations

Your faith has healed you. Go in peace and be freed from your suffering. Mark 5:34 (NIV)

Affirmations: I have faith that God can heal me and remove this pain. I choose to think peaceful, calming thoughts. I can think about Jesus' compassion and how he healed people.

Write your own affirmations:

_____

_____

_____

Receive your sight; your faith has healed you. Luke 18:42 (NIV)

Affirmations: My faith can heal me.

Write your own affirmations:

_____

_____

_____

I will restore you to health and heal your wounds. Jeremiah 30:17 (NIV)

Affirmations: I believe God heals illnesses and injuries. He can restore my health. I can relax and trust him and thank him in advance for health and healing.

Write your own affirmations:

_____

_____

_____

Whatever is true, whatever is noble, whatever is right, whatever is pure, whatever is lovely, whatever is admirable — if anything is excellent or praiseworthy — think about such things. Philippians 4:8 (NIV)

Affirmations: I think and talk about things that are good, lovely, and admirable, *especially* when I'm in pain. I avoid thinking about things I can't do, and I think about things that I *can* do. Even before the pain stops, I will thank God for healing me.

Write your own affirmations:

_____

_____

_____

A cheerful heart is good like medicine. Proverbs 17:22 (TLB)

Affirmations: I can smile and speak cheerfully because I know it's a potent remedy. I believe that hope and happiness will help me. I can take a dose of cheerfulness each day. I know my thoughts and speech have power, and I wisely use that power.

Write your own affirmations:

Pleasant sights and good reports give happiness and health. Proverbs 15:30 (TLB)

Affirmations: I take time to enjoy nature, or pictures of it. I share uplifting stories and encouraging news. I avoid talking needlessly about pain.

Write your own affirmations:

Speak to these bones for me. Tell them, "Dry bones, listen to the word of the Lord! This is what the Lord God says to you: I will cause breath to come into you, and you will come to life!" Ezekiel 37: 4 (ERV)

Affirmations: I breathe deeply to help heal my body. I will imagine pain being dissolved and exhaled from my body.

Write your own affirmations:

_____

_____

_____

Gentle words cause life and health. Proverbs 15:4 (TLB)

Affirmations: I speak tenderly to myself when I'm sick. I tell my body to get well. And I firmly tell illness to go away. Gentleness to myself and others can make me feel loved. And it moves me forward when I feel discouraged.

Write your own affirmations:

_____

_____

_____

Chapter 8

Comfort vs. Loneliness

After my son-in-law earned his graduate degree, I left Massachusetts and relocated *again* with the family – now including three little ones – to a small town near the University of Michigan. A couple of months later, I did something I knew was wrong. I worked far beyond my physical limits and then did more work and errands. Later that night, I took a walk, and I was too tired to tighten my shoelace. When I stumbled and hit the sidewalk, I knew I'd broken my knee.

As I waited in the emergency room, I managed the pain with prayer and deep breathing. The fracture did not require surgery, only a leg brace, physical therapy, and prayer. Two months later, the fracture had healed, and I was walking without the leg brace.

But during the tenth week after my injury, I would experience the most painful and the longest night of the year.

December 21 – Yalda Night – is a holiday in some countries. In Iranian communities around the world, friends gather to spend the darkest night together, laughing and eating foods that remind them brighter days are coming. When I lived in Los Angeles, I celebrated Yalda with my Muslim friend, Homa.

On this Yalda Night in Michigan, my youngest sister called me. Our conversation drifted toward a time when we had some serious disagreements. She asked me to talk about them to improve our relationship. I briefly explained, and she kindly apologized. Then she asked for more instances so she could apologize further. I felt cautious and suggested that we may be opening a can of worms.

Years earlier, my older sister Kris had given me a wonderful lesson on forgiveness. "Honey, don't go back and review all the arguments. Just forgive each other for what the person did and forgive yourself for what you may have done. Start all over now."

When my younger sister repeated her question about past issues, my intuition said, "Don't explain." But I didn't listen to my intuition, and I started to explain. I spoke carefully, trying to avoid conflict. Fortunately, I had to leave the house, and the call ended quickly.

But the conversation didn't stop there. It lit a fire in my brain. The more I recalled, the more I seethed. The more I felt self-righteous, the more I ignored memories of times that I had offended her also. I planned what I'd do: I'd go home, eat dinner, call my sister, and let her know what I was *really* thinking.

As I was standing in my kitchen – *simply standing* – my previously injured knee buckled. Suddenly the top of my leg slid backward, and the bottom part of my leg slid forward. I slammed onto the floor. The pain was excruciating.

I called the hospital emergency room, and the nurse gave me some instructions and suggested that I stay home. They were swamped. I should see my orthopedist in the morning. My daughter and neighbors stopped by to help.

Unlike the night when I'd fractured my kneecap, I couldn't manage this pain. I couldn't sleep. I could barely pray. I was off kilter. *This* was the longest night of my year. And I felt alone.

As I recalled how angry I had been feeling, I realized that a lot of adrenaline was flooding through my body. I was ready to attack. But maybe my attack backfired. Could my high adrenaline have been related to an intense knee-jerk reflex?

In any case, I made an emphatic mental note to stop ruminating about our past offenses with each other and go back to loving and *for-giving*.

* * *

As my knee healed a second time, I stayed at home during the day and wrote for my client. At night, I struggled with loneliness. I knew that I needed social connections to prevent depression.[1] And I missed having access to the people, places, and things that were familiar.

When I lived in other cities, I'd often visit friends, neighbors, or people in the nursing home where my sister Patty lived. Those visits made me feel loved and linked to others. But I was new in this town, so I prayed I would find someone who needed a friend.

That winter as I recovered, I often opened my curtains at night and watched the snow, stars, fog, or barren trees. The utter beauty was breathtaking and filled me with a sense of God's greatness. Frequently, the loneliness I had felt would melt into comfort and a connection to a greater Presence.

One day when I was hobbling inside a store, an elderly British woman started a conversation with me. Christine invited me to her home for tea and initiated other visits. She called just to check-in and helped me get adjusted to the new town, often introducing me to her friends. She was a blessing – God's love with an English accent.

* * *

Since that time, there has been another relocation and challenges after leaving friends and neighbors. But the best midnight comfort – when it's too late to call loved ones in any city – has always occurred when I've connected with God by praying or appreciating the beauty of his creation.

Chapter 8: Comfort vs. Loneliness

Related Science

A comprehensive analysis of 148 research studies involving more than 300,000 participants showed that having social connections helped people to survive health problems. This 2010 study was led by Julianne Holt-Lunstad and published in *PLOS Medicine*. The study was titled "Social relationships and mortality risk: A meta-analytic review."

* * *

A team of researchers studied international students and found that when adequate social support was not available, meaningful activities could reduce loneliness and improve well-being and cognitive health. This 2022 study was led by Liang-Chih Chang and published in *Leisure Sciences*. The study was titled "Relationships of leisure social support and flow with loneliness in international students in Taiwan."

* * *

In a study involving 1,200 older adults in two different cultures, researchers found that receiving either emotional support or receiving help with housekeeping, finances, and transportation was shown to protect against loneliness. The 2014 study was led by Marta M. Sanchez Rodrigues and published in *Aging and Society*. The study was titled "Loneliness and the exchange of social support among older adults in Spain and the Netherlands."

Dear Reader,

The path to deeper relationships may be well-traveled,

Or bypassed.

Deceptive self-righteousness can publicly console –

And privately mock fallen travelers.

Repairing old friendships and growing new friendships will lure sleeping flowers into full bloom.

Dormancy ends, youth is revived.

When deep truth sparks vulnerability in the night, we can dance in the day.

And on Hope Street – the music is sweet.

Rosie

113

Chapter 8: Comfort vs. Loneliness

Inspiration and Affirmations

Come near to God and he will come near to you. James 4:8 (NIV)

Affirmations: I can talk with God and write to him. I can think about God being close to me in my home, in my car, and in my office. I believe that God is near me.

Write your own affirmations:

_____

_____

_____

Though my father and mother forsake me, the Lord will receive me. Psalms 27:10 (NIV)

Affirmations: I know that God never abandons me. Even if my friends and loved ones are not with me, God will welcome me and comfort me.

Write your own affirmations:

_____

_____

_____

A father to the fatherless, a defender of widows, is God in his holy dwelling. Psalm 68:5 (NIV)

Affirmations: I can imagine that God is with me. When I feel lonely or upset, I can think about him helping me, directing me, or defending me.

Write your own affirmations:

_____

_____

_____

When you are praying, first forgive anyone you are holding a grudge against, so that your Father in heaven will forgive you your sins too. Mark 11:24 (TLB)

Affirmations: I forgive people who hurt me. And I trust God to provide me with the things that I need.

Write your own affirmations:

_____

_____

_____

Chapter 9

Rest vs. Overwork

With five kids, my mom always had plenty to do. But on Sundays, she would say, "No servile work!"

That meant, after church we would help prepare meals and wash dishes. Then we could watch movies or play. Sundays were a respite from housework and schoolwork.

Years passed. I forgot those habits and sometimes worked every day of the week, including weekends. In my thirties, a co-worker who was Jewish told me she spent the Sabbath relaxing, reading, eating, and visiting. She looked so refreshed on Mondays. I was jealous!

I wondered why I didn't think I should do that, too. I had the same Ten Commandments: No murder, no stealing, no lying, etc. Why was it OK to eliminate the most fun one? Rest on Sunday!

Gradually, I wove rest into my Sundays. When I was a married mom with two little girls, I found ways to reduce the workload. I'd cook extra food on Saturday, serve easy meals on Sundays, and plan to work or do errands on the other days.

I'm sure that anticipating a day to *really* rest each week triggered the reward circuit in my brain and increased dopamine, providing a little natural propellent to prepare for my upcoming break.

Some of the best Sundays were when my family and I would go hiking in the Santa Monica Mountains. My husband would notice families who were having picnics and "doing it right."

They'd bring lots of food, listen to music, play games, and stay at the park all day – not just a couple of hours like we did. I wanted to do that, too.

Circumstances changed. Later as a busy single mom with school-aged daughters, I seldom took them to the mountains. Then, my day of rest started any time – on a Friday night, Saturday, or Sunday. I was just grateful to carve out 24 hours for self-care and a connection to God.

Years later, my daughter would ask me what I wanted to do for my birthday. The answer was always the same: Let's have a picnic!

Another year when she asked, I told her I wanted an *all-day* picnic. With her, my son-in-law, and my three grandchildren, we spent *seven* whole hours on Sunday relaxing by a lake, eating, napping, talking, and laughing. It was wonderful. We got it right!

That night, I was so happy that I could barely fall asleep. I kept thanking God for a full day of rest with my loved ones while basking in the beauty of his nature.

Time passed and when my other daughter returned from her worldwide travels, my choice for a picnic would still be the same – but my joy was exponential because she was there, too.

* * *

When I had a weekend alone, I experienced a strong reference point for deep rest. I'd been working for a radio station, sometimes doing remote broadcasts on Saturday. Exhausted from work and stressful life events, I knew I had to do something to help myself.

One Friday evening when my daughters went to visit their dad, I turned off my computer and stopped checking messages. I lit candles and ate a good dinner with chicken soup and healthy comfort foods.

For the next 24 hours, I rested and spent *lots* of time doing the relaxation response.[1] That meant breathing deeply, pausing, and slowly exhaling while silently repeating a comforting phrase. I chose words from scripture. Sometimes I'd imagine exhaling tension or pain. Naturally, my heart rate slowed, and I felt less tension.

The next day, I took slow walks, listened to peaceful classical music, and read a sweet romance novel. By Sunday afternoon, I was amazed to feel absolutely rejuvenated.

There was no cost for my little vacation, and the physical and emotional benefits were astounding. That weekend became my gold standard for complete self-compassion and a reconnection with God.

* * *

Over time, I've found a way to enjoy a short Sabbath or rejuvenation time every day. About an hour before bedtime, I reduce visual and audio stimulation. I stop looking at my computer and phone. Lights go dim. I listen to very slow music or enjoy the silence. After I wash and prepare for bed, I do slow exercises to reduce my heart rate.

Next, I talk to God about my day – what I'm grateful for, what went right, what went wrong, what I regret, and what I can do to change.

Perceiving God as a friend helps me to share my deepest thoughts and feelings. Sincerely talking about my shortcomings with God reduces stress. Planning better ways to handle difficult situations relaxes me. Finally, asking God for help and thanking him in advance gives me hope.

It's not necessary to make this a fancy prayer time. This is a time to be honest and vulnerable and enjoy a relationship with a friend.

I bless my loved ones and those whose behavior troubles me. I climb into bed, and briefly read one of Jesus' teachings, jotting it in a notebook and thinking of ways to apply it to my life. Last, I often re-read little bits of an old, relaxing novel by a kind-hearted Scottish author, George MacDonald. Then lights go out, and I breathe deeply to further relax.[2]

Chapter 9: Rest vs. Overwork

Related Science

Diaphragmatic breathing, or deep breathing, can significantly reduce cortisol and stress. In addition, diaphragmatic breathing was shown to improve the ability to pay attention and focus. The 2017 study was led by Xiao Ma and published in *Frontiers in Psychology*. The study was titled "The effect of diaphragmatic breathing on attention, negative affect and stress in healthy adults."

* * *

Researchers found that resting for just 10 minutes after learning new information helped participants retain detailed information. The absence of other sensory information appears to strengthen new memory systems. The 2018 study was led by Michael Craig and published in *Scientific Reports*. The study was titled "Rest-related consolidation protects the fine detail of new memories."

* * *

Working long hours may have a negative effect on memory and reasoning abilities. In a study of more than 2,000 participants, researchers found that working 55 hours or more per week was associated with lower scores on a vocabulary test, and it reduced abilities on a reasoning test. The 2009 study led by Marianna Virtanen was published in the *American Journal of Epidemiology*. The study was titled "Long Working Hours and Cognitive Function: The Whitehall II Study."

* * *

During an experiment done by the Boston Consulting Group, consultants found that professionals who had a strict system of taking evenings off and one day off each week had more positive perceptions of their work circumstances than their peers who were not in the experiment. Also, the participants showed improved learning, open communication, and better product development. The 2009 article by Leslie A. Perlow and Jessica L. Porter was published in the *Harvard Business Review*. The article was titled "Making Time Off Predictable – and Required."

* * *

Learning and new memories are consolidated in the hippocampus, which functions best when a person has a full night's sleep. The 2007 study was led by Seung-Schik Yoo and published in *Nature Neuroscience*. The study was titled "A deficit in the ability to form new human memories without sleep."

* * *

A study involving nearly 20,000 subjects showed that spending an accumulated total of two hours in nature each week can benefit health, cognition, and well-being. When people feel safe in parks, green spaces, or other natural environments, the time spent in nature can lower blood pressure, reduce stress hormones, enhance immune function, and provide other health benefits. The 2019 study was led by Mathew P. White and published in *Scientific Reports*. The study was titled "Spending at least 120 minutes a week in nature is associated with good health and wellbeing."

Dear Reader,

We can choose to wrap ourselves in simple pleasures –

healing and breathing the preciousness of self-compassion.

Uninvited distractions can be silenced, submitting to human strength.

Why do we wait? For time? For money? For space?

Our mortal birthright for rest can be renewed each day, each week, sometime, somewhere –

But always along Hope Street.

Rosie

Chapter 9: Rest vs. Overwork

Inspiration and Affirmations

My presence will go with you, and I will give you rest. Exodus 33:14 (NIV)

Affirmations: I can picture God with me as I rest. He can help me sleep and restore my soul.

Write your own affirmations:

_____

_____

_____

Rest in the Lord; wait patiently for him to act. Psalms 37:7 (TLB)

Affirmations: I breathe deeply as I imagine God and rest. I trust him to help me with my problems after I rest.

Write your own affirmations:

_____

_____

_____

It is useless for you to work so hard from early morning until late at night, anxiously working for food to eat; for God gives rest to his loved ones. Psalm 127:2 (NLT)

Affirmations: I take short breaks during my workday, and I rest in the evening. I try to work calmly, take care of problems, and refuse to worry. I know that God can help me rest at night.

Write your own affirmations:

_____

_____

_____

I lay down and slept in peace and woke up safely, for the Lord was watching over me. Psalms 3:5 (NIV)

Affirmations: I can think about God watching over me as I lie down to sleep. I can tell myself that I will sleep peacefully and safely because God cares for me.

Write your own affirmations:

_____

_____

_____

Come to me, all you who are weary and burdened, and I will give you rest. Take my yoke upon you and learn from me, for I am gentle and humble in heart, and you will find rest for your souls. For my yoke is easy and my burden is light. Matthew 11:28 (NIV)

Affirmations: I imagine giving my worries and problems to God. I trust God to teach me to be gentle and honest and forgiving. I believe he helps me to rest.

Write your own affirmations:

_____

_____

_____

Epilogue

Hope

N euroscientist Eric Kandel told me *all* living things require hope for survival. But sometimes we hope and fervently pray, and important prayers don't get answered. Still, I can't ignore all the times when God has helped me. And I can't ignore the encouraging words from Jesus: Ask for anything, believe, persist, forgive, confess, love, abide, thank, and receive.

When prayers aren't answered, I still have the choice to connect with God and honestly express my grief, anger, confusion, or disappointment. I can still ask for answers and comfort. From those times of intimacy, change occurs. Adjustments are made. Guidance is perceived. And the door remains open for hope.

* * *

A few years ago, I visited Los Angeles for a special gathering of family and friends. As I waited outside the airport terminal for my ride, I recalled other arrivals and departures in California. During that hour, the sights and smells triggered memories and emotions – love, bliss, anger, sadness, and grief. They were the emotions associated with nearly four decades of my life. I had to re-organize myself.

I chose to use gratitude. I thanked God for all the blessings and all the life I had experienced in California, for all the people who had been a special part of my life, and for all the breath-taking gifts of nature. As I did that, the mist of sadness disappeared. Gratitude gently turned into hope.

Afterword

During challenging times, dark times, and war times, there are always people around the world who show kindness or love through an act of courage or generosity or even a warm smile. They create a beam of light on Hope Street. To them, I say thank you.

Spring 2022

Prayer for Peace

This prayer is attributed to Saint Francis of Assisi. It was common during World War 1 and World War 11.

Lord, make me an instrument of your peace.

Where there is hatred, let me bring love.

Where there is offence, let me bring pardon.

Where there is discord, let me bring union.

Where there is error, let me bring truth.

Where there is doubt, let me bring faith.

Where there is despair, let me bring hope.

Where there is darkness, let me bring your light.

Where there is sadness, let me bring joy.

O Master, let me not seek as much to be consoled as to console,

to be understood as to understand,

to be loved as to love,

for it is in giving that one receives,

it is in self-forgetting that one finds,

it is in pardoning that one is pardoned,

it is in dying that one is raised to eternal life.

Dear Reader,

Here's a parting message for you:

Keep hope alive – for something, for anything.

Hope feels better than despair,

And gratitude to God can feel the best.

Testing ideas, testing faith –

we're all on this journey together –

as we walk, or stumble, or crawl, or run, or dance along Hope Street.

Love,

Rosie

Appendix

- Find Reliable Health Information

- Research Shortcuts

- Questions for Study Groups

- Recommended Reading and Viewing

- Action Steps

- Notes

- Acknowledgements

- About the Author

Find Reliable Health Information

I hope this book has sparked a greater interest in research. Here are some helpful tips for finding reliable information about health, medicine, or science.

Start at the top of the money trail. People pay taxes to the U.S. government. Then the National Institutes of Health (NIH) provides money to universities, research institutions, and medical centers to pay for specific research.

When research is complete, scientists and researchers write articles about their discoveries. Their articles are submitted to medical or scientific journals. The articles are reviewed by peers who analyze and scrutinize the research.

If an article is approved for publication, a news release may be written. The news release will be approved by the researchers. The news release is published on the website of the university, medical center, or research institute. Also, the news is sent to the NIH for their website. The research will be included in updated articles for consumers on MedlinePlus.gov and the Center for Disease Control.

To make the research known quickly to the public, press releases are sent to news organizations and journalists. Editors review the information and decide whether or not to write an article or produce a news segment about the research. News reports will depend on the importance or timeliness of the research, current trends, and other factors.

Health organizations, associations and foundations use the news releases to inform patients, caregivers, and others.

Companies and corporations use the news releases to inform investors and stimulate interest in new products.

Educators, authors, and public speakers refer to the research in their lessons, presentations, and books. Other people post information about the research on their websites and in blogs or videos.

As the information filters down the line, or as it is recycled, it may contain small or large errors – like those errors that occur when people play the game "telephone." People whisper a message in another person's ear, only to learn that the original message was altered a little or a lot.

When you have questions about research – or supposed research – look for a news release or an article. Read the original journal article about the research. For difficult words, use the online dictionary.

Happy hunting!

Research Shortcuts

Here are some shortcuts for online health research:

- Use keywords and National Institutes of Health

- Use keywords and the name of a leading university that does medical research.

- Use keywords and the name of a well-known or established health organization, association, or foundation. For example, the American Cancer Society.

- Use keywords and include "news release" and the current or previous year.

- Use keywords and the names of organizations that distribute press releases, such as ScienceDaily or Newswise.

- Use keywords and include "scholarly articles." Plan to use the online dictionary to look up new words.

- Use keywords and include the word "abstract." An abstract is a brief summary of a research article in a journal.

Enjoy learning!

Questions for Study Groups

How did the information in this book relate to what you already knew about faith or brain science?

What misconceptions did you have about faith or brain science?

What did you gain from reading this book?

What information have you already used from this book?

What additional information would you like to use?

Who else could be helped by the ideas in this book?

How could you pray for people who upset you?

What were your experiences with thinking traps?

What activities make you feel connected to God?

What are some of your experiences that relate to neuroplasticity?

What ideas from this book might help you in the future?

Who can you share this information with?

Recommended Reading and Viewing

How God Changes Your Brain, by Andrew Newberg, M.D. and Mark Robert Waldman. Related videos are available on YouTube.

The Brain That Changes Itself, by Norman Doidge, M.D. Related videos are available on YouTube.

Cured: The Life-Changing Science of Spontaneous Healing, by Jeffrey Rediger, M.D. Related videos are available on YouTube.

Timeless Healing: The Power and Biology of Belief, by Herbert Benson, M.D. Related videos are available on YouTube.

Wiser: Getting Beyond Groupthink to Make Groups Wiser, by Cass R. Sunstein and Reid Hastie. Related videos are available on YouTube.

In Search of Memory: The Emergence of a New Science of Mind, by Eric R. Kandel, M.D. Related videos are available on YouTube.

The Language of God: A Scientist Presents Evidence for Belief, by Francis S. Collins, M.D. Related videos are available on YouTube.

Unbelievable? Why, After Ten Years of Talking With Atheists, I'm Still a Christian, by Justin Brierley. Related videos are available on YouTube.

Action Steps

Consider re-reading sections of this book to help you recall what you've learned and continue to practice the affirmations.

We are not all the same, but we are not all alone. If you need resources or professional help, please look for it. You deserve goodness and support. God bless all your efforts.

Here are some useful websites:

- Association for Anxiety and Depression: www.adaa.org

- Association for Behavioral and Cognitive Therapies: www.abct.org

- HelpGuild provides free mental health education and support: www.helpguide.org.

- National Suicide Prevention Lifeline: 1-800-273-TALK (8255)

* * *

Notes

Forward

1. Doidge, N. (2007). *The Brain That Changes Itself: Stories of Personal Triumph from the Frontiers of Science.* Penguin Life.

2. Llies, R., Wagner, D. T., et al. (2007). Explaining affective linkages in teams: individual differences in susceptibility to contagion and individualism–collectivism. *Journal of Applied Psychology,* 92(4):1140-1148.

3. Cohen, S., Doyle, W. J., et al. (2003). Emotional style and susceptibility to the common cold. *Psychosomatic Medicine,* 65(4):652-657.

4. Fournier, M., de Ridder, D., et al. (2002). How optimism contributes to the adaptation of chronic illness. A prospective study into the enduring effects of optimism on adaptation moderated by the controllability of chronic illness. *Personality and Individual Differences,* 33(7):1163-1183.

5. Bevy, B. R., Slade, M. D., et al. (2018). Positive age beliefs protect against dementia even among elders with high-risk gene. *PLOS ONE,* 13(2): e0191004.

6. Kandel, E. (2007). *In Search of Memory: The Emergence of a New Science of Mind.* W.W. Norton & Company, Inc.

Introduction and Explainer

1. Kandel, E. (2007). *In Search of Memory: The Emergence of a New Science of Mind.* W.W. Norton & Company, Inc.

2. Master, S. L., Eisenberger, N. I., et al. (2009). A picture's worth: Partner photographs reduce experimentally induced pain. *Psychological Science,* 20(11): 1316-1318.

3. Filkowski, M. M., Cochran, R. N., et al. (2016). Altruistic behavior: Mapping responses in the brain. *Neuroscience Neuroeconomics,* 5: 65-75.

4. Lawler, K. A., Younger, J. W., et al. (2005). The unique effects of forgiveness on health: An exploration of pathways. *Journal of Behavioral Medicine.* 28(2): 157-167.

5. Watkins, P.C., Woodward, K., et al. (2003). Gratitude and happiness: Development of a measure of gratitude, and relationship with subjective well-being. *Social Behavior and Personality,* 31(5): 431-452.

6. Algoe, S., Haidt, J., et al. (2008). Beyond reciprocity: Gratitude and relationships in everyday life. *Emotion,* 8, 425-429.

7. Kashdan, T., Uswatte, G., et al. (2006). Gratitude and hedonic and eudaimonic well-being in Vietnam war veterans. *Behaviour Research and Therapy,* 44(2): 177-199.

8. Krause, N., Pargament, K. I., et al. (2016). Humility, stressful life events, and psychological well-being: Findings from the landmark spirituality and health survey. *Journal of Positive Psychology,* 11:5, 499-510.

9. Bellucci, G., Molter F., et al. (2019). Neural representations of honesty predict future trust behavior. *Nature Communications,* 10, 5184.

10. Hekman, D. R. (2012). Modeling how to grow: An inductive examination of humble leader behaviors, contingencies, and outcomes. *Academy of Management Journal,* 55(4), 787-818.

11. Bromberg-Martin, E. S., Matsumoto, M., et al. (2010). Dopamine in motivational control: Rewarding, aversive, and alerting. *Neuron,* 68(5): 815-834.

12. Salamone, J. D. and Correa, M. (2012). The mysterious motivational functions of mesolimbic dopamine. *Neuron,* 76(3): 470.

13. Inzlicht, M., McGregor, I., Hirsh, J. B., et al. (2009). Neural markers of religious conviction. *Psychological Science,* 20(3): 385.

14. Benson, H., Beary, J. F., et al. (1974). The relaxation response. *Psychiatry,* 37:1, 37-46.

15. Forrin, N. D. and MacLeod, C. M. (2018). This time it's personal: The memory benefit of hearing oneself. *Memory,* 26(4): 574-479.

16. Strasser, A., Luksys, G., et al. (2020). Glutamine-to-glutamate ratio in the nucleus accumbens predicts effort-based motivated performance in humans. *Neuropsychopharmacology,* 45, 2048-2057.

Chapter 1: Kindness vs. Harshness

1. Barraza, J. A., and Zak, P. J. (2009). Empathy toward strangers triggers oxytocin release and subsequent generosity. *Annals of the New York Academy of Sciences,* June;1167:182-189.

2. Young, C. B., and Nusslock, R. (2016). Positive mood enhances reward-related neural activity. *Social Cognitive and Affective Neuroscience,* 11(6), 934-944.

Chapter 2: Forgiveness vs. Anger

1. Worthington, Jr., E. L., Van Oyen Witvliet, C., et al. (2007). Forgiveness, health, and well-being: A review of evidence for emotional versus decisional forgiveness, dispositional forgiveness, and reduced unforgiveness. *Journal of Behavioral Medicine,* 30(4): 291-302.

2. Worthington, Jr., E. L., Van Oyen Witvliet, C., et al. (2007). Forgiveness, health, and well-being: A review of evidence for emotional versus decisional forgiveness, dispositional forgiveness, and reduced unforgiveness. *Journal of Behavioral Medicine,* 30(4): 291-302.

Chapter 3: Gratitude vs. Bitterness

1. Watkins, P. C., Woodward, K., et al. (2003). Gratitude and happiness: Development of a measure of gratitude and relationships with subjective well-being. *Social Behavior and Personality: An International Journal,* 31(5), 431-452.

Chapter 4: Truth vs. Deception

1. Janis, I. (1991). *Groupthink.* McGraw-Hill.

2. Ferguson, M. A., Schaper, F., et al. (2021). A neural circuit for spirituality and religiosity derived from patients with brain lesions. *Biological Psychiatry,* 91(4): 380-388.

Chapter 5: Persistence vs. Quitting

1. Stephens, R., Atkins, J., et al. (2009). Swearing as a response to pain. *NeuroReport,* 20(12): 1056-1060.

2. Gold, P. E. (2014). Regulation of memory – from the adrenal medulla to liver to astrocytes to neurons. *Brain Research Bulletin,* 105: 25-35.

3. Kell, C. A., et al. (2009). How the brain repairs stuttering. *Brain,* 132(10): 2747-2760.

4. Hebb, D. O. *The Organization of Behavior: A Neuropsychological Theory.* John Wiley & Sons, Ltd., 1949.

5. Song, S., Miller, K. D., et al. (2000). Competitive Hebbian learning through spike-timing dependent synaptic plasticity. *Nature Neuroscience,* 3: 919-926.

6. Alderson-Day, B. and Fernyhough, C. (2015). Inner speech: Development, cognitive functions, phenomenology, and neurobiology. *Psychological Bulletin Journal,* 141(5): 931-965.

7. Perrone-Bertolotti, M., Rapin, et al. (2014). What is that little voice in my head? Inner speech phenomenology, its role in cognitive performance, and its relation to self-monitoring. *Behavioural Brain Research,* 261:220-239.

8. Liu, P. Z. and Nusslock, R. (2018). Exercise-mediated neurogenesis in the hippocampus via BDNF. *Frontiers in Neuroscience,* 12:52.

Chapter 6: Courage vs. Fear

1. Clandos, R. (2008, September 1). Too stressed out to learn. *Los Angeles Times.*

2. Giles, G. E., Horner, C. A., et al. (2020). When anger motivates: Approach states selectively influence running performance. *Frontiers in Psychology.* August. doi.org/10.3389/fpsyg.2020.01663

Chapter 7: Healing vs. Pain

1. Ferguson, M. A., Schaper, F., et al. (2021). A neural circuit for spirituality and religiosity derived from patients with brain lesions. *Biological Psychiatry,* 91(4): 380-388.

2. Conversano, C., Rotondo, A., et al. (2010). Optimism and its impact on mental and physical well-being. *Clinical Practice & Epidemiology in Mental Health.* 6:25-29.

3. Redinger, J. (2020). *Cured: The life-changing science of spontaneous healing.* Flatiron Books.

4. Corsi, N. and Colloca, L. (2017). Placebo and nocebo effects: The advantage of measuring expectations and psychological factors. *Frontiers in Psychology.* March. www.frontiersin.org/articles/10.3389/fpsyg.2017.00308/full

Chapter 8: Comfort vs. Loneliness

1. Choi, K. W., Stein, M. B., et al. (2020). An exposure-wide and Mendelian randomization approach to identifying modifiable factors for the prevention of depression. *American Journal of Psychiatry.* August. doi.org/10.1176/appi.ajp.2020.19111158

Chapter 9: Rest vs. Overwork

1. Bhasin, M. K., Dusek, J. A., et al. (2013). Relaxation response induces temporal transcriptome changes in energy metabolism, insulin secretion and inflammatory pathways. *PLOS ONE.* 8(5): e62817.

2. Zaccaro, A., Piarulli, A., et al. (2018). How breath-control can change your life: A systematic review on psycho-physiological correlates of slow breathing. *Frontiers in Human Neuroscience,* 12: 353.

Acknowledgements

I am most grateful to God for guidance, peace, and hope.

Thanks also goes to early editors Sue Hudson and Terry Hassman-Paulin. Special thanks to June Abramian for astute content editing in the revised version of this book.

I deeply appreciate the support of my friends Pam Fazalare, Val Rope, Eileen Richmond, and Duane and Linda Wilson.

I am grateful for my dear daughters Elizabeth Clandos and Christina Guiley. They encouraged me to stop using bullet points to describe my past and start disclosing. Thanks to Elizabeth for broad perspective, feedback, and encouragement. Thanks to Christina for diplomatic suggestions, portrait photography, and content editing.

I thank my four sisters: Kris Khurana and Dolores Wylie for support and input. To Barbara Morrish, thanks for listening to my doubts about God and offering your viewpoint. To Patty Zoladz, thank you for a life lived with faith, curiosity, and great courage.

Thanks goes to Christopher Guiley, Gary Morrish, and all those who cheered for me, especially in the final stretch. Thanks to Christina Jen Photography for the portrait.

With heartfelt gratitude, I thank Ellen Freeman. When my mom was on hospice, I received a picture of Ellen reading a section of this book to my mom. I learned Ellen did this often. The image motivated me to finish writing the book so people of all ages and all backgrounds might benefit from the peace that comes with increased knowledge and hope.

About the Author

Rosie Clandos has written about cancer research, molecular pathology, nanobiotechnology, microelectromechanical systems, and other science-related topics. While working as a research assistant in a brain electrophysiology lab, she wrote about cognition and informed consent for patients with traumatic brain injury. For the *Los Angeles Times*, she wrote about subjects ranging from music and business to science. As a contract writer for a media production company, she worked on projects for the U.S. Department of Defense and the National Science Foundation.

Rosie was raised Catholic near an industrial area of Detroit. At age 18, she walked away from the church and gradually became an agnostic. After life-changing events, she developed a personal relationship with God and experienced greater power from prayer and renewed faith. Over the years and in many different cities, her faith has been strongly influenced by people of different racial and ethnic groups.

Rosie continues to write for universities, researchers, and medical centers. Now, she lives in Oregon – within walking distance of her three grandchildren.

Contact Rosie at RosemaryClandos@gmail.com Learn more at www.RosemaryClandos.com

"Tell me, what is it you plan to do

with your one wild and precious life?"

~ Mary Oliver ~

.

Made in the USA
Columbia, SC
16 August 2022

65081378R00090